STING

THE ILLUSTRATED LYRICS

ROBERTO GLIGOROV | **STING**

I.R.S. BOOKS

LOS ANGELES LONDON

DESIGN FOR UNITED STATES PUBLICATION: F RON MILLER.

ISBN 1-879510-00-6

CONTENTS

ROBERTO GLIGOROV was born in December of 1959, in the town of Kriva Palanka, Yugoslavia. His father was a builder, his mother an actress dancer whose career was interrupted by the birth of two children.

The family broke up and Roberto went to live with foster parents, a farmer and his wife on the island of Brac.

He left Yugoslavia at the age of nine and, reunited with his mother, went to live in Italy in the city of Venice. He spoke no Italian, which of course created a few problems for Roberto and the priests who taught him. Roberto sought solace in the language of drawing. The artistic impulse seems to be a way of dealing with limitations, linguistic and emotional; can art only flourish in the maladjusted, the misfit, the loner?

Roberto slowly assimilated himself and began to study chemistry seriously, to please his mother he claims, but in each spare moment day or night he would draw, enrolling in an art college at night after school. He was now living in Milan and was a champion diver, chosen to represent Italy in international competition, but there was a problem — Roberto was still legally a Yugoslav.

At 20 he went to Rome to get somehow into the art world. He tried acting, modeling, photography, anything to pay the rent; meanwhile, those who saw his artwork told him he had no talent, to go back to diving. The rejection only hardened his resolve to become an artist. He worked and studied for 5 years, abandoning the company of his critics. When he returned after his exile, the transformation in his art was so striking that no one would believe he had done the work himself.

More and more he began to use music as an inspiration for his work — Italian opera, Beethoven, etc. — but occasionally he would try to express visually the images of pop songs.

The influence of the art schools on the pop music of the '60's is well-documented;   in Gligorov's case the influence worked the other way, the pop music of the '80's becoming his visual territory.

 In 1983, Gligorov encountered a serious problem; people began to mistake him for me, stopping him in the street, asking for his auto-graph, tearing his clothes.

I first met him backstage at the Teator Tenda, a circus tent in Milan where I was giving a con-cert. Everyone thought he was me, although he's much better looking than I am, he looks the way I ought to look, like a projection of me; no one bothers me when Roberto's in the room. I think I like it.

Anyway, I can't draw and he can't sing, so we have a symbiotic relationship. The more I get to know him, the closer to me he seems; his life is painted in different colours than mine but it has the same shape, the same awkward and compelling perspectives.

I hope you like the book as much as I do, and that you will enjoy hearing my songs through his eyes.

Love,

Sting

GS/JRW

All this time

I looked out across
the river today
I saw a city in the fog and an old church tower
where the seagulls play
I saw the sad shire horses walking home
in the sodium light
I saw two priests on the ferry
october geese on a cold winter's night

And all this time, the river flowed
endlessly to the sea

Two priests came round our house tonight
one young, one old, to offer prayers for the dying
to serve the final rite,
one to learn, one to teach,
which way the cold wind blows
fussing and flapping in priestly black
like a murder of crows
And all this time the river flowed
endlessly to the sea
If I had my way I'd take a boat from the river
and I'd bury the old man,
I'd bury him at sea

Blessed are the poor, for they shall inherit the earth
better to be poor than a fat man in the eye of a needle
and as these words were spoken I swear I hear
the old man laughing
what good is a used up world, and how could it be
worth having.

And all this time the river flowed
endlessly like a silent tear
And all this time the river flowed
father, If Jesus exists,
then how come he never lived here

The teachers told us, the romans built this place
they built a wall and a temple an edge of the empire
Garrison town,
they lived and they died, they prayed to their gods
but the stone gods did not make a sound
and their empire crumbled, 'til all that was left
were the stones the workmen found

And all this time the river flowed
in the falling light of a northern town
If I had my way I'd take a boat from the
river

men go crazy in congregations
but they only get better
one by one
one by one...

All this time

JEREMIAH BLUES (PART 1)

IT WAS MIDNIGHT, MIDNIGHT AT NOON

EVERYONE TALKED IN RHYME

EVERYONE SAW THE BIG CLOCK TICKING

NOBODY KNEW, NOBODY KNEW THE TIME

ELEGANT DEBUTANTES SMILED

EVERYONE FOUGHT FOR DIMES

NEWSPAPERS SCREAMED FOR BLOOD

IT WAS THE BEST OF TIMES

EVERY PLACE AROUND THE WORLD IT SEEMED THE SAME...

CAN'T HEAR THE RHYTHM FOR THE DRUMS

EVERYBODY WANTS TO LOOK THE OTHER WAY

WHEN SOMETHING WICKED THIS WAY COMES

SOMETIMES THEY TIE A THIEF TO THE TREE

SOMETIMES I STARE

SOMETIMES IT'S ME

EVERYONE TOLD THE TRUTH

ALL THAT WE HEARD WERE LIES

A POPE CLAIMED THAT HE'D BEEN WRONG IN THE PAST

THIS WAS A BIG SURPRISE

EVERYONE FELL IN LOVE

A CARDINAL'S WIFE WAS JAILED

THE GOVERNMENT SAVED A DYING PLANET

WHEN POPULAR ICONS FAILED

EVERY PLACE AROUND THE WORLD IT SEEMED THE SAME

CAN'T HEAR THE RHYTHM FOR THE DRUMS

EVERYBODY WANTS TO LOOK THE OTHER WAY

WHEN SOMETHING WICKED THIS WAY COMES

SOMETIMES THEY TIE A THIEF TO THE TREE

SOMETIMES I STARE

SOMETIMES IT'S ME

SOMETIMES I STARE

SOMETIMES IT'S ME

Island of Souls

BILLY WAS BORN WITHIN SIGHT OF THE SHIPYARD
FIRST SON OF A RIVETER'S SON
BILLY WAS RAISED AS THE SHIP GREW A SHADOW
HER GREAT HULL WOULD BLOT OUT THE LIGHT OF THE SUN. AND SIX DAYS A WEEK HE WOULD WATCH HIS POOR FATHER. A WORKING MAN LIVE LIKE A SLAVE. HE'D DRINK EVERY NIGHT AND HE'D DREAM OF A FUTURE, OF MONEY HE NEVER WOULD SAVE. AND BILLY WOULD CRY WHEN HE THOUGHT OF THE FUTURE SOON CAME A DAY WHEN THE BOTTLE WAS BROKEN. THEY LAUNCHED THE GREAT SHIP OUT TO SEA. HE FELT HE'D BEEN LEFT ON A DESOLATE SHORE. TO A FUTURE HE DESPERATELY WANTED TO FLEE. WHAT ELSE WAS THERE FOR A RIVETER'S SON? A NEW SHIP TO BE BUILT, NEW WORK TO BE DONE. ONE DAY HE DREAMED OF THE SHIP IN THE WORLD IT WOULD CARRY HIS FATHER AND HE TO A PLACE THEY COULD NEVER BE FOUND, TO A PLACE FAR AWAY FROM THIS TOWN. TRAPPED IN THE CAGE OF THE SKELETON SHIP. ALL THE WORKMEN SUSPENDED LIKE FLIES. CAUGHT IN THE FLARE OF ACETYLENE LIGHT. A WORKING MAN WORKS TILL THE INDUSTRY DIES. AND BILLY WOULD CRY WHEN HE THOUGHT OF THE FUTURE. THEN WHAT THEY CALL AN INDUSTRIAL ACCIDENT, CRUSHED THOSE IT COULDN'T FORGIVE. THEY BROUGHT BILLY'S FATHER BACK HOME IN AN AMBULANCE A BRASS WATCH, A CHEQUE, MAYBE THREE WEEKS TO LIVE AND WHAT ELSE WAS THERE FOR A RIVETER'S SON A NEW SHIP TO BE BUILT, NEW WORK TO BE DONE. THAT NIGHT, HE DREAMED OF THE SHIP IN THE WORLD. IT WOULD CARRY HIS FATHER AND HE TO A PLACE THEY COULD NEVER BE FOUND. TO A PLACE FAR AWAY FROM THIS TOWN, A NEWCASTLE SHIP WITHOUT COALS. THEY WOULD SAIL TO THE ISLAND OF SOULS.

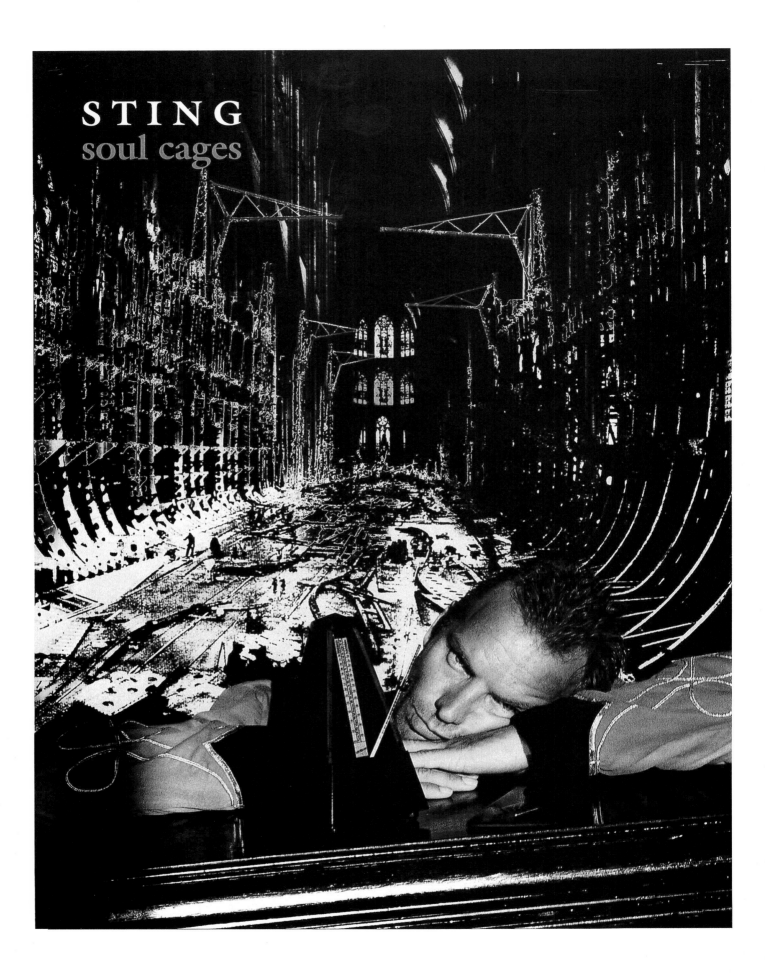

STING
soul cages

STING

soul cages

The boy child is locked in the fisherman's yard
There's a bloodless moon where the oceans die
A shoal of nightstars hang fire in the nets
and the chaos of cages where the crayfish lie

Where is the fisherman, where is the goat?
Where is the keeper in his carrion coat?
Eclipse on the moon when the dark bird flies
Where is the child with his father's eyes?

These are the soul cages   These are the soul cages

He's the king of the ninth world
The twisted son of the fog bells toll
In each and every lobster cage
A tortured human soul

These are the souls of the broken factories
The subject slaves of the broken crown
The dead accounting of old guilty promises
These are the souls of the broken town

These are the soul cages   These are the soul cages
These are the soul cages   These are the soul cages

'I have a wager' the brave child spoke
The fisherman laughed, though disturbed at the joke.
'You will drink what I drink but you must equal me
And if the drink leaves me standing,
   a soul shall go free'

'I have here a cask of most magical wine'
A vintage that blessed every ship in the line
It's wrung from the blood of the sailors who died
Young white bodies adrift in the tide

'And what's in it for me my pretty young thing?
Why should I whistle, when the caged bird sings?
If you lose a wager with the king of the sea
You'll spend the rest of forever in the cage with me'

These are the soul cages   These are the soul cages
These are the soul cages   These are the soul cages

A body lies open in the fisherman's yard
Like the side of a ship where the iceberg rips
One less soul in the soul cages
One last curse on the fisherman's lips

These are the soul cages   These are the soul cages
These are the soul cages   These are the soul cages

Swim to the light   Swim to the light

He dreamed of the ship on the sea
It would carry his father and he
To a place they could never be found
To a place far away from this town
A Newcastle ship without coals
They would sail to the Island of Souls

THE WILD WILD SEA

I saw it again this evening,
black sail in a pale yellow sky
and just as before in a moment,
it was gone where the grey gulls fly.

If it happens again I shall worry
that only a strange ship could fly
and my sanity scans the horizon
in the light of a darkening sky.

That night as I walked in my slumber
I waded into the sea strand
and I swam with the moon and her lover
until I lost sight of the land.

I swam till the night became morning
black sail in a reddening sky
found myself on the deck of a rolling ship
so far where no grey gulls fly.

All around me was silence
as if mocking my frail human hopes
and a question mark hung in the canvas
for the wind that had died in the ropes.

I may have slept for an hour
I may have slept for a day
for I woke in a bed of white linen
and the sky was the color of clay.

At first just a rustle of canvas
and the gentlest breath on my face
but a galloping line of white horses
said that soon we were in for a race.

The gentle sigh turned to a howling
and the grey sky she angered to black
and my anxious eyes searched the horizon
with the gathering sea at my back.

Did I see the shade of a sailor
on the bridge through the wheelhouse pane
held fast to the wheel of the rocking ship
as I squinted my eyes in the rain.

For the ship had turned into the wind
against the storm to brace
and underneath the sailor's hat
I saw my father's face.

If a prayer today is spoken
please offer it for me
when the bridge to heaven is broken
and you're lost on the wild wild sea
lost on the wild wild sea...

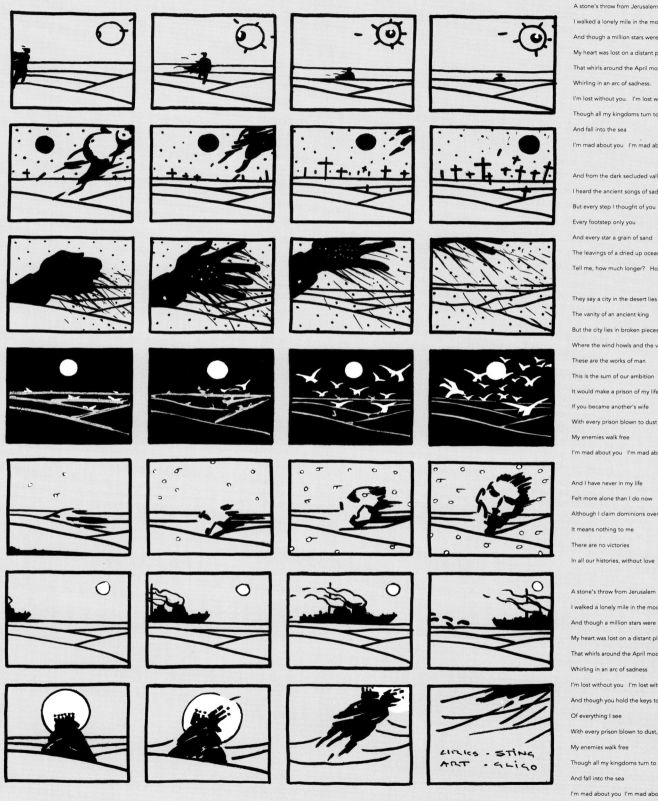

A stone's throw from Jerusalem

I walked a lonely mile in the moonlight

And though a million stars were shining

My heart was lost on a distant planet

That whirls around the April moon

Whirling in an arc of sadness.

I'm lost without you. I'm lost without you.

Though all my kingdoms turn to sand

And fall into the sea

I'm mad about you   I'm mad about you

And from the dark secluded valleys

I heard the ancient songs of sadness

But every step I thought of you

Every footstep only you

And every star a grain of sand

The leavings of a dried up ocean

Tell me, how much longer?   How much longer?

They say a city in the desert lies

The vanity of an ancient king

But the city lies in broken pieces

Where the wind howls and the vultures sing

These are the works of man

This is the sum of our ambition

It would make a prison of my life

If you became another's wife

With every prison blown to dust

My enemies walk free

I'm mad about you   I'm mad about you

And I have never in my life

Felt more alone than I do now

Although I claim dominions over all I see

It means nothing to me

There are no victories

In all our histories, without love

A stone's throw from Jerusalem

I walked a lonely mile in the moonlight

And though a million stars were shining

My heart was lost on a distant planet

That whirls around the April moon

Whirling in an arc of sadness

I'm lost without you   I'm lost without you

And though you hold the keys to ruin

Of everything I see

With every prison blown to dust,

My enemies walk free

Though all my kingdoms turn to sand

And fall into the sea

I'm mad about you   I'm mad about you

WHEN THE ANGELS FALL

SO HIGH ABOVE THE WORLD TONIGHT

THE ANGELS WATCH US SLEEPING

AND UNDERNEATH A BRIDGE OF STARS

WE DREAM IN SAFETY'S KEEPING

BUT PERHAPS THE DREAM

IS DREAMING US

SOARING WITH THE SEAGULLS

PERHAPS THE DREAM

IS DREAMING US

ASTRIDE THE BACKS OF EAGLES

WHEN THE ANGELS FALL

SHADOWS ON THE WALL

IN THE THUNDER'S CALL

SOMETHING HAUNTS US ALL

WHEN THE ANGELS FALL

WHEN THE ANGELS FALL

TAKE YOUR FATHER'S CROSS

GENTLY FROM THE WALL

A SHADOW STILL REMAINING

SEE THE CHURCHES FALL

IN MIGHTY ARCS OF SOUND

AND ALL THAT THEY'RE CONTAINING

YET ALL THE

RAGGED SOULS

OF ALL THE RAGGED MEN

LOOKING FOR THEIR LOST HOMES

SHUFFLE TO THE RUINS

FROM THE LEVELLED PLAIN

TO SEARCH AMONG

THE TOMBSTONES

WHEN THE ANGELS FALL
SHADOWS ON THE WALL
IN THE THUNDER'S CALL
SOMETHING HAUNTS US ALL

WHEN THE ANGELS FALL
WHEN THE ANGELS FALL
WHEN THE ANGELS FALL

THESE ARE MY FEET
THESE ARE MY HANDS
THESE ARE MY CHILDREN
AND THIS IS MY DEMAND
BRING DOWN THE ANGELS
CAST THEM FROM MY SIGHT
I NEVER WANT TO SEE
A MILLION SUNS AT MIDNIGHT

YOUR HANDS ARE EMPTY
THE STREETS ARE EMPTY
YOU CAN'T CONTROL US
YOU CAN'T CONTROL US ANYMORE

WHEN THE ANGELS FALL
WHEN THE ANGELS FALL
WHEN THE ANGELS FALL

WHEN THE ANGELS FALL
WHEN THE ANGELS FALL
WHEN THE ANGELS FALL

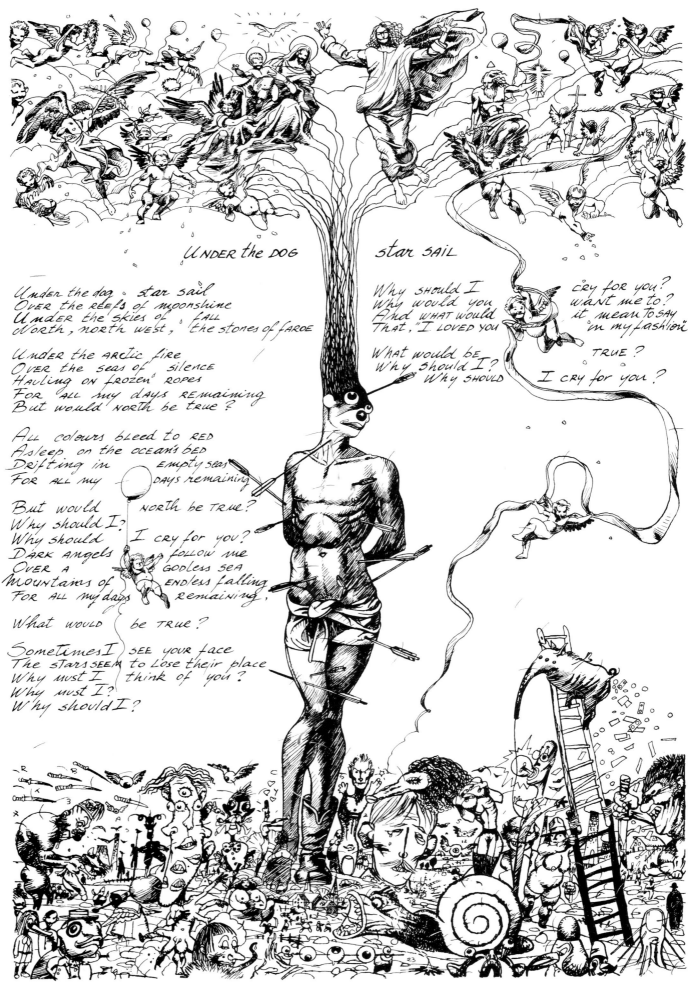

UNDER the DOG · star SAIL

Under the dog · star sail
Over the reefs of moonshine
Under the skies of · fall
North, north west, · the stones of faroe

Under the arctic fire
Over the seas of · silence
Hauling on frozen ropes
For all my days remaining
But would north be true?

All colours bleed to red
Asleep on the ocean's bed
Drifting in · empty seas
For all my · days remaining

But would · north be true?
Why should I?
Why should · I cry for you?
Dark angels · follow me
Over a · godless sea
Mountains of · endless falling
For all my days · remaining,

What would · be true?

Sometimes I · see your face
The stars seem to lose their place
Why must I · think of you?
Why must I?
Why should I?

Why should I
Why would you
And what would
That, "I loved you

What would be
Why should I?
Why should

cry for you?
want me to?
it mean to say
in my fashion

TRUE?

I cry for you?

13

Gordon Matthew Sumner

Napoleon

(HISTORY) WILL TEACH US NOTHING

If we seek solace in the
    prisons of the distant past
Security in human systems
we're told will always last
Emotions are the sail and blind
faith is the mast
Without the breath of real freedom
we're getting nowhere fast

Mendel

Josif Stalin

Fellini

Edgar Allan Poe

Sting

George A. Custer

Francisco Villa

Robespierre

Karl Gustav Jung

14

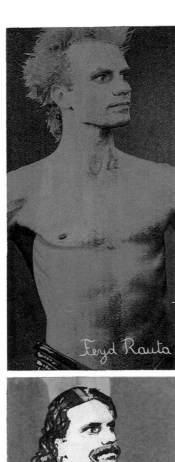

Feyd Rauta

Jesus Christ

Adolf Hitler

If God is dead and an actor plays his part
His words of fear will find their way to a place in your heart
Without the voice of reason every faith is its own curse
Without freedom from the past things can only get worse
Sooner or later just like the world first day
Sooner or later we learn to throw the past away
Sooner or later just like the world first day
Sooner or later we learn to throw the past away
Sooner or later we learn to throw the past away
History will teach us nothing
History will teach us nothing

Wild B. Hickok

Benito Mussolini

Oliver North

Jewish

St. Francesco

Sting

Mahatma Gandhi

Nerone

15

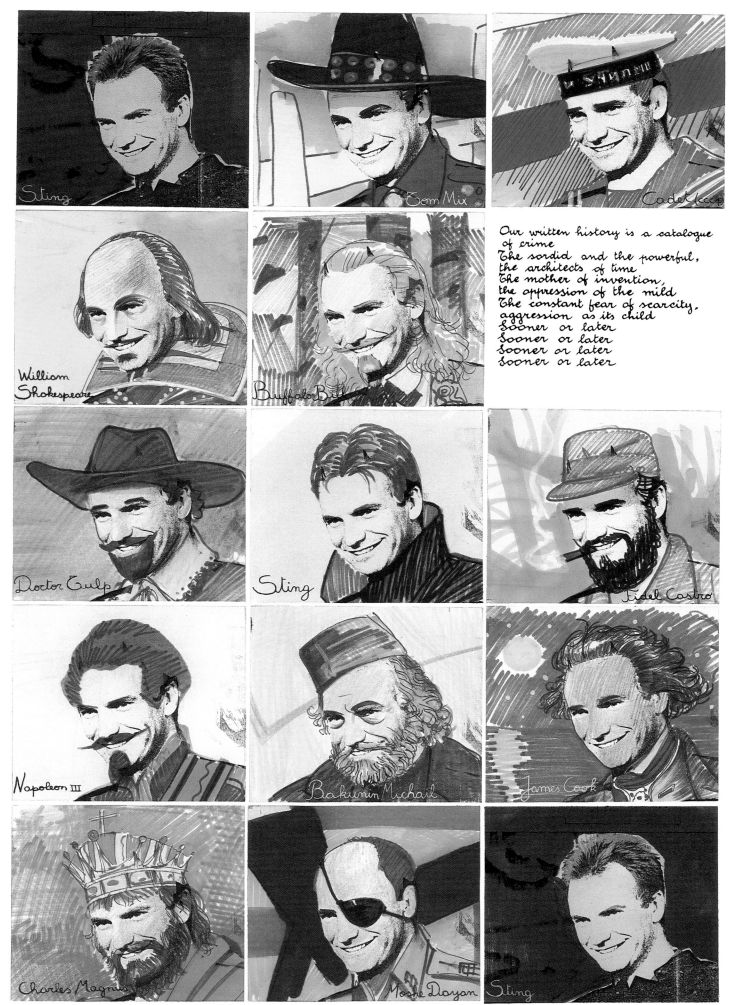

Sting

Tom Mix

Cadet Keep

William Shakespeare

Buffalo Bill

Our written history is a catalogue
of crime
The sordid and the powerful,
the architects of time
The mother of invention,
the oppression of the mild
The constant fear of scarcity,
aggression as its child
Sooner or later
Sooner or later
Sooner or later
Sooner or later

Doctor Gulp

Sting

Fidel Castro

Napoleon III

Bakunin Michail

James Cook

Charles Magnus

Moshe Dayan

Sting

16

Andy Warhol

Sting

J. Bach

Antonio Gramsci

Rasputin

Jerome

Kafka

Giuseppe Verdi

Marlene Dietrich

Sting

Convince an enemy, convince him that he's wrong
Is to win a bloodless battle where victory is long
A simple act of faith
In reason over might
To blow up his children will only prove him right
History will teach us nothing
Sooner or later just like the world first day
Sooner or later we learn to throw the past away
Sooner or later just like the world first day
Sooner or later we learn to throw the past away
Sooner or later we learn to throw the past away

Martina

Bette Davis

Salvador Dali

Baby

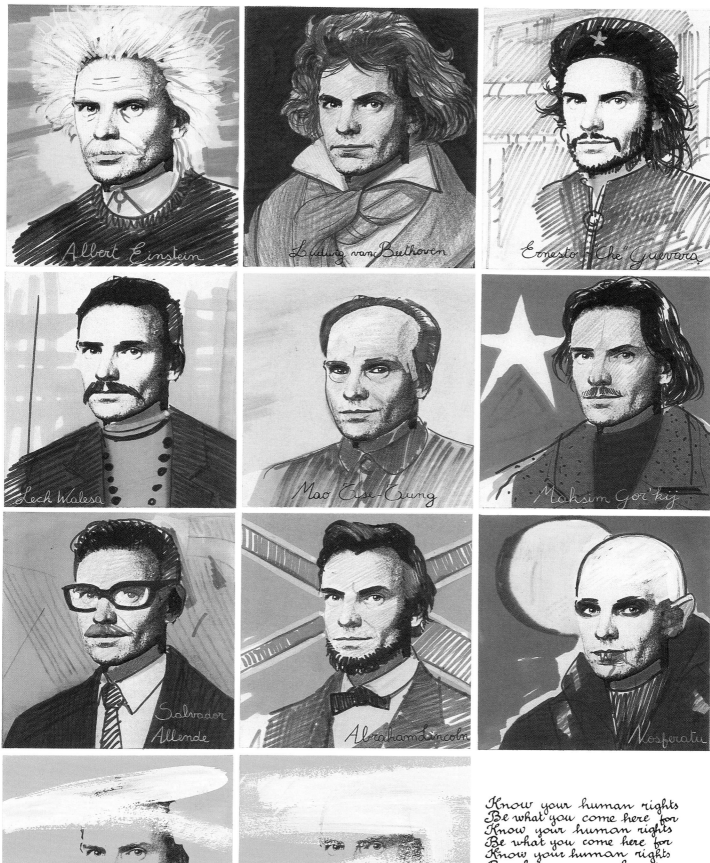

Albert Einstein

Ludwig van Beethoven

Ernesto "Che" Guevara

Lech Walesa

Mao Tse-Tung

Maksim Gor'kij

Salvador Allende

Abraham Lincoln

Nosferatu

History will teach us nothing

History will teach us nothing

Know your human rights
Be what you come here for
Know your human rights
Be what you come here for
Know your human rights
Be what you come here for
Know your human rights
Be what you come here for

Sister moon
will be my guide
in your blue blue
shadows I would
hide. All good
peoples asleep
tonight I'm all
by myself in
your silver light
I would gaze at
your face the
whole night,
through I'd go
out of my mind
but for you
lying in a mother's
arms the primal
root of a
woman's charms
I'm a stranger
to the sun
My eyes are too
weak how cold
is a heart when
it's warmth that
he seek?
You watch every
night, you don't
care what I do
I'd go out of my
mind, but for you
I'd go out of my
mind, but for you
My mistress's
eyes are
nothing like
the sun. My
hunger for her
explains everything
I've done to howl
at the moon the
whole night through.

SISTER MOON

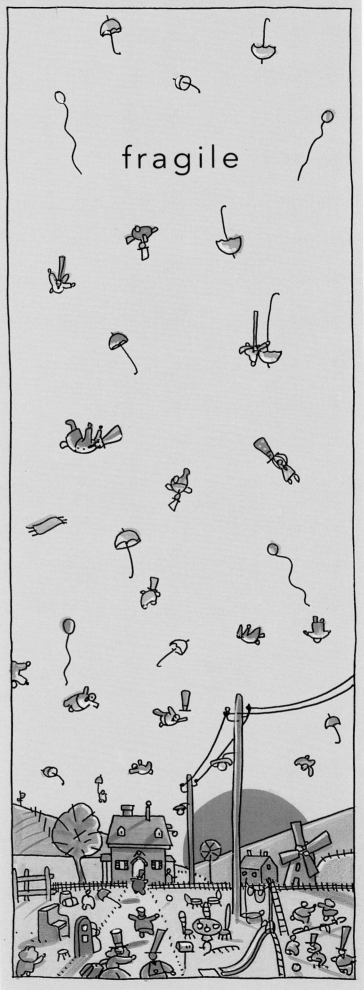

fragile

For all those born beneath
an angry star
Lest we forget how fragile we are

On and on the rain will fall
Like tears from a star
On and on the rain will say
How fragile we are

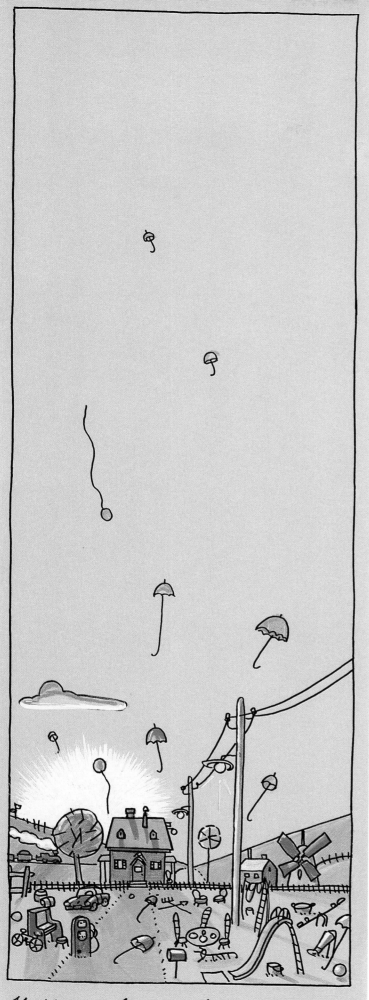

If blood will flow when flesh and steel are one
Drying in the colour of the evening sun
Tomorrow's rain will wash the stains away
But something in our minds will always stay

Perhaps this final act was meant
To clinch a lifetime's argument
That nothing comes from violence
and nothing ever could

SECRET MARRIAGE

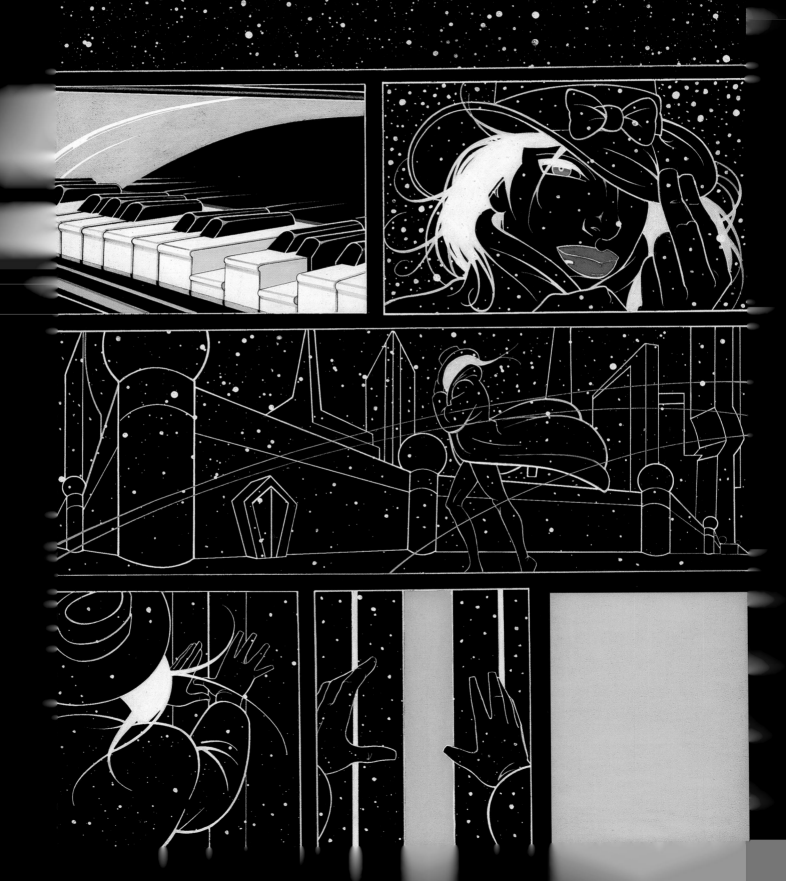

NO EARTHLY CHURCH HAS EVER BLESSED OUR UNION
NO STATE HAS EVER GRANTED US PERMISSION

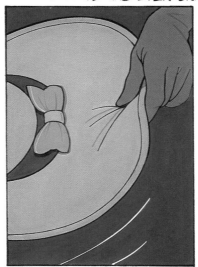

NO FAMILY BOND HAS EVER MADE US TWO

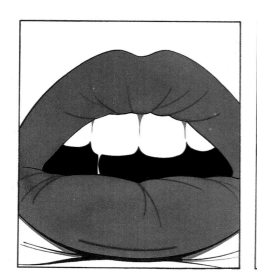

NO COMPANY HAS EVER EARNED COMMISSION

NO DEBT WAS PAID NO DOWRY TO BE GAINED

NO TREATY OVER BORDER LAND OR POWER
NO SEMBLANCE OF THE WORLD OUTSIDE REMAINED

TO STAIN THE BEAUTY OF THIS NUPTIAL HOUR

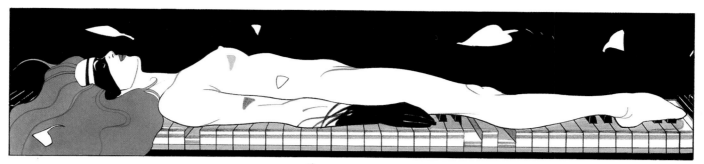

THE SECRET MARRIAGE VOW IS NEVER SPOKEN

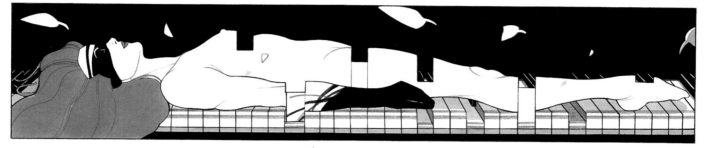

THE SECRET MARRIAGE NEVER CAN BE BROKEN

NO FLOWERS ON THE ALTAR

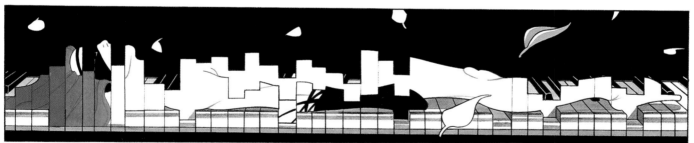

NO WHITE VEIL IN YOUR HAIR

NO MAIDEN DRESS TO ALTER

NO BIBLE OATH TO SWEAR

THE SECRET MARRIAGE VOW IS NEVER SPOKEN

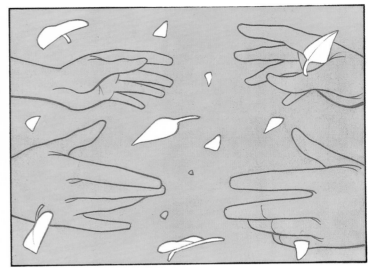

THE SECRET MARRIAGE NEVER CAN BE BROKEN

ENGLISHMAN IN NEW YORK

STING

I DON'T DRINK COFFEE I TAKE TEA MY DEAR

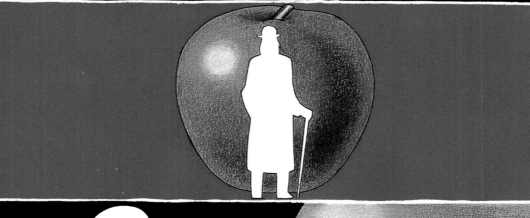

I LIKE MY TOAST DONE ON THE SIDE

AND YOU CAN HEAR IT IN MY ACCENT WHEN I TALK I'M AN ENGLISHMAN IN NEW YORK

SEE ME WALKING DOWN FIFTH AVENUE A WALKING CANE HERE AT MY SIDE

I TAKE IT EVERYWHERE I WALK I'M AN ENGLISHMAN IN NEW YORK

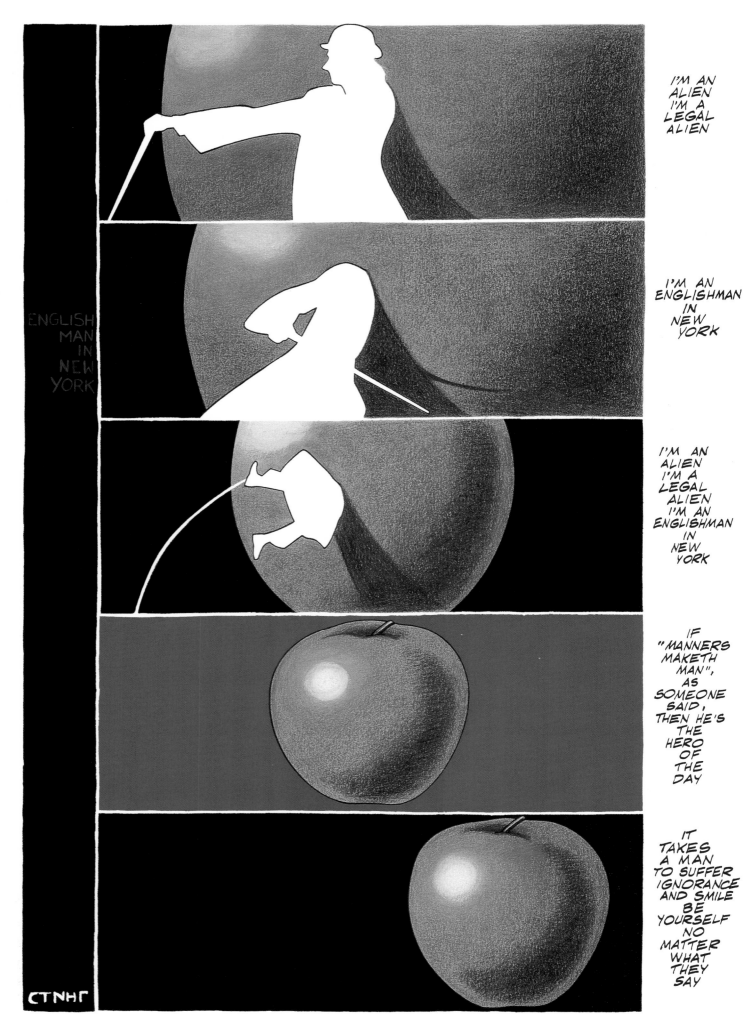

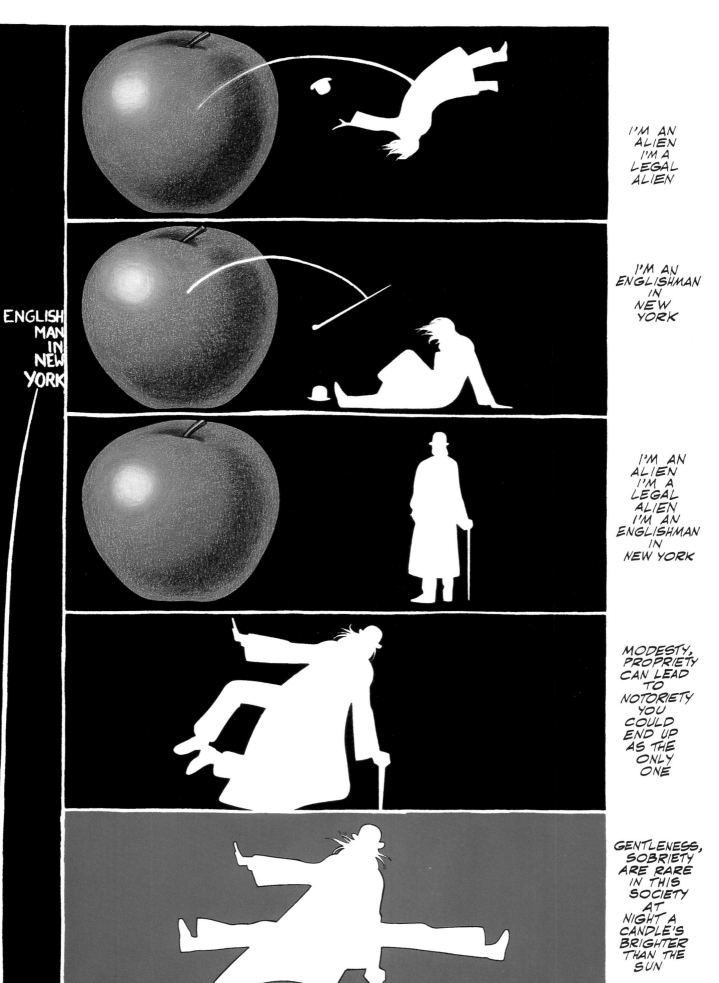

30

TAKES
MORE
THAN
COMBAT
GEAR TO
MAKE
A MAN
TAKES
MORE
THAN A
LICENSE
FOR A
GUN
CONFRONT
YOUR
ENEMIES,
AVOID
THEM
WHEN
YOU
CAN

A
GENTLEMAN
WILL
WALK BUT
NEVER
RUN

IF
"MANNERS
MAKETH
MAN",
AS
SOMEONE
SAID,

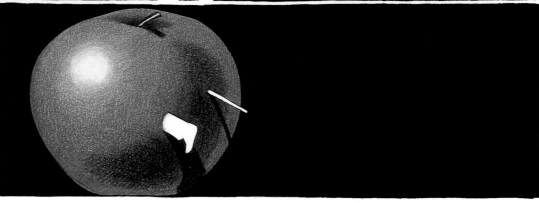

THEN
HE'S THE
HERO
OF THE
DAY

Englishman in New York

STING

31

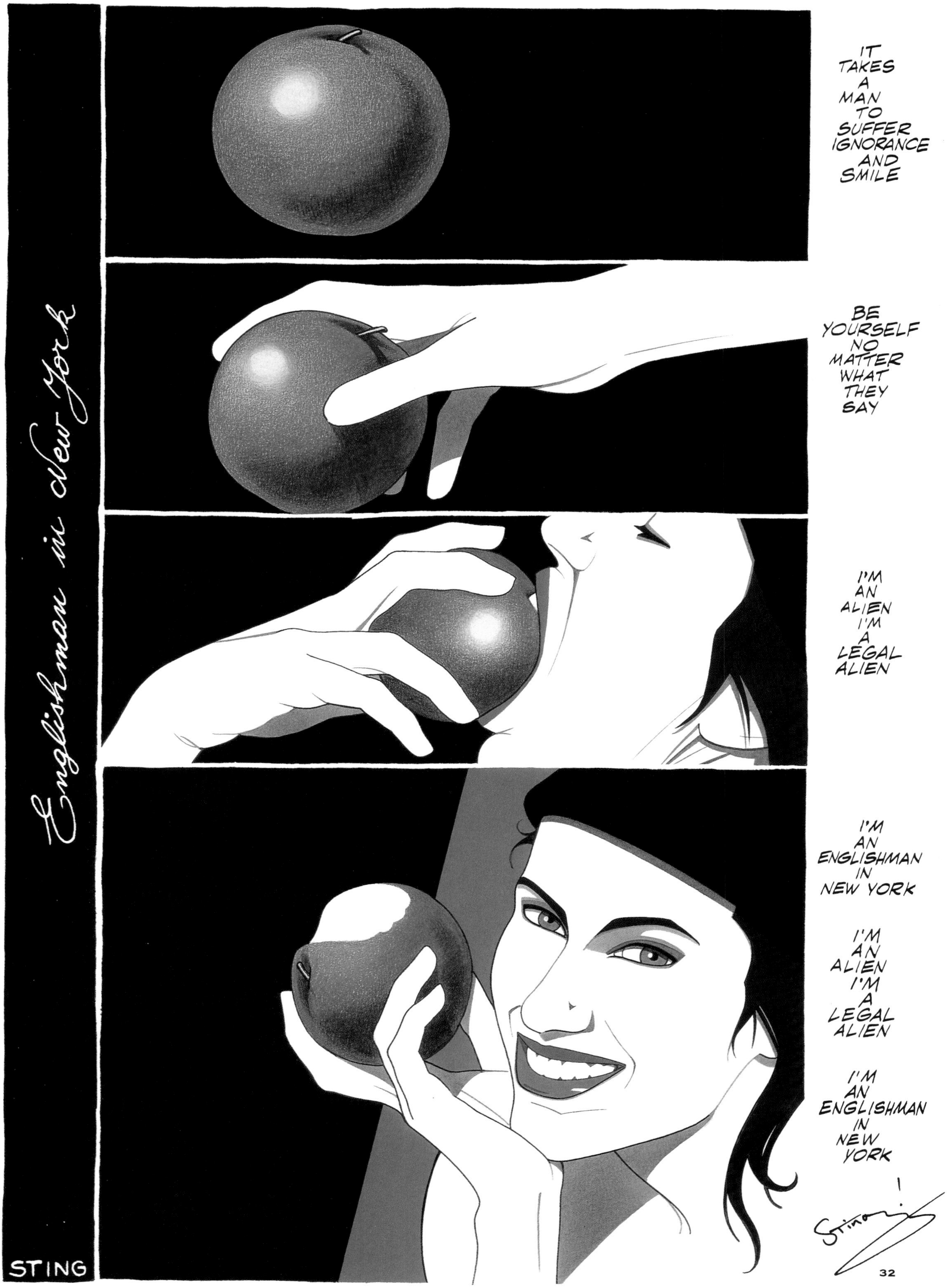

Englishman in New York

STING

IT TAKES A MAN TO SUFFER IGNORANCE AND SMILE

BE YOURSELF NO MATTER WHAT THEY SAY

I'M AN ALIEN I'M A LEGAL ALIEN

I'M AN ENGLISHMAN IN NEW YORK

I'M AN ALIEN I'M A LEGAL ALIEN

I'M AN ENGLISHMAN IN NEW YORK

32

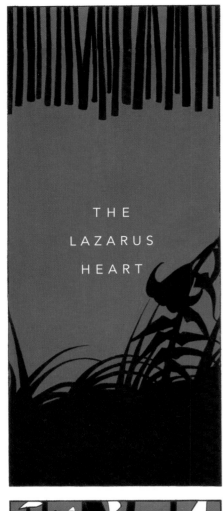

THE
LAZARUS
HEART

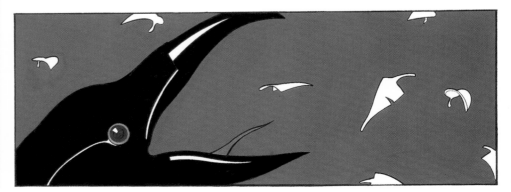

[H]E LOOKED BENEATH HIS SHIRT TODAY
    THERE WAS A WOUND IN HIS FLESH SO DEEP AND WIDE
FROM THE WOUND A LOVELY FLOWER GREW

FROM SOMEWHERE DEEP INSIDE
HE TURNED AROUND TO FACE HIS MOTHER

TO SHOW HER THE WOUND IN HIS BREAST THAT BURNED LIKE A BRAND

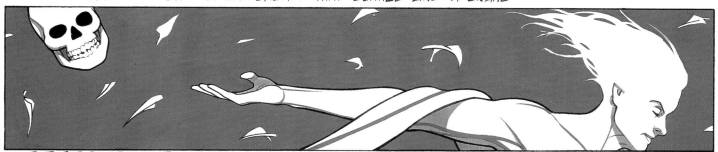

BUT THE SWORD THAT CUT HIM OPEN
WAS THE SWORD IN HIS MOTHER'S HAND

EVERY DAY ANOTHER MIRACLE
NOT EVEN DEATH COULD TEAR US APART

TO SACRIFICE A LIFE FOR YOURS
I'D BE THE BLOOD OF THE LAZARUS HEART
THE BLOOD OF THE LAZARUS HEART

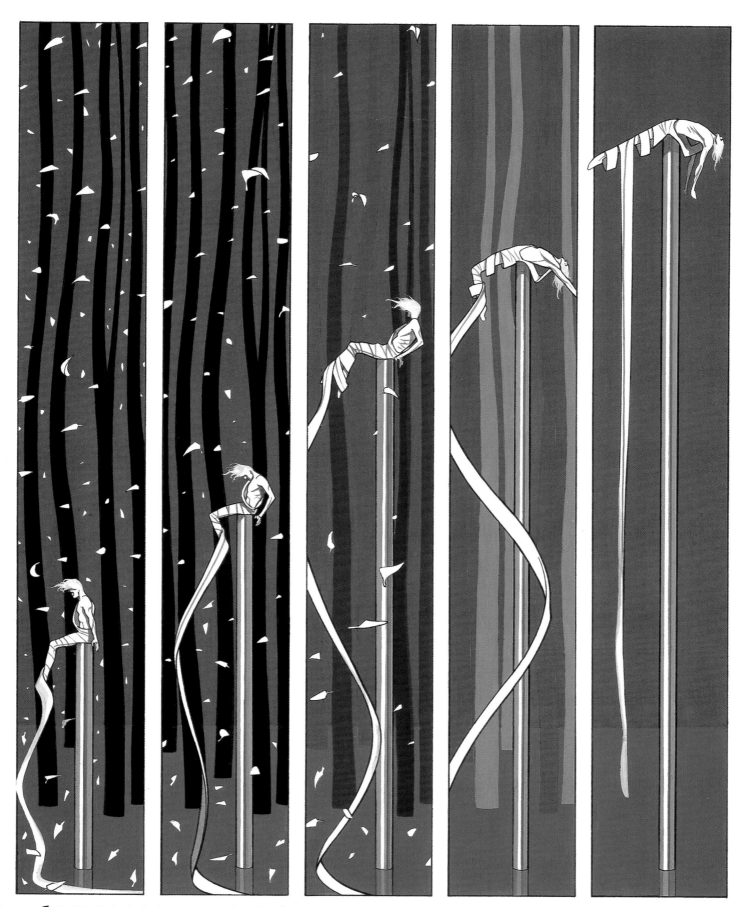

THOUGH THE SWORD WAS HIS PROTECTION
THE WOUND ITSELF WOULD GIVE HIM POWER
THE POWER TO REMAKE HIMSELF AT THE TIME OF HIS DARKEST HOUR
SHE SAID THE WOUND WOULD GIVE HIM COURAGE AND PAIN
THE KIND OF PAIN THAT YOU CAN'T HIDE
FROM THE WOUND A LOVELY FLOWER GREW
FROM SOMEWHERE DEEP INSIDE

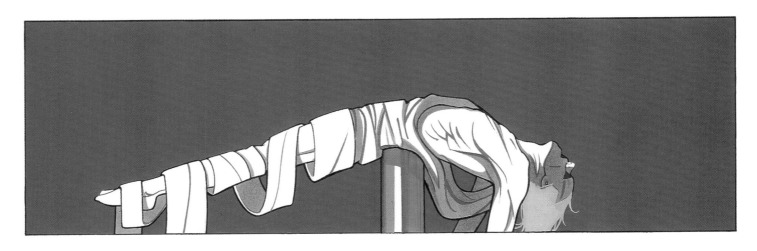

EVERY DAY ANOTHER MIRACLE
NOT EVEN DEATH COULD KEEP US APART
TO SACRIFICE A LIFE FOR YOURS
I'D BE THE BLOOD OF THE LAZARUS HEART
THE BLOOD OF THE LAZARUS HEART

BIRDS ON THE ROOF OF MY MOTHER'S HOUSE
I'VE NO STONES THAT CHASE THEM AWAY
BIRDS ON THE ROOF OF MY MOTHER'S HOUSE

WILL SIT ON MY ROOF SOMEDAY
THEY FLY AT THE WINDOW, THEY FLY AT THE DOOR

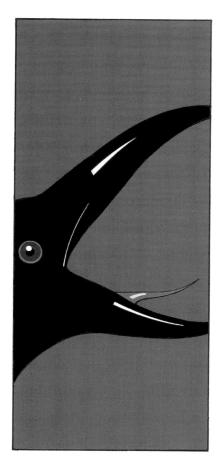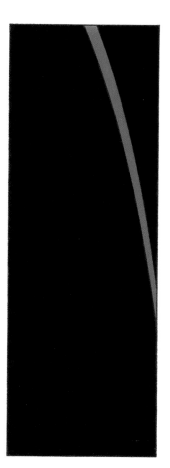

WHERE DOES SHE GET THE STRENGTH TO FIGHT THEM ANYMORE
SHE COUNTS ALL HER CHILDREN AS A SHIELD AGAINST THE PAIN

LIFTS HER EYES TO THE SKY LIKE A FLOWER TO THE RAIN !
EVERY DAY ANOTHER MIRACLE
NOT EVEN DEATH COULD KEEP US APART
TO SACRIFICE A LIFE FOR YOURS
I'D BE THE BLOOD OF THE LAZARUS HEART
THE BLOOD OF THE LAZARUS HEART

38

STRAIGHT
TO
MY HEART

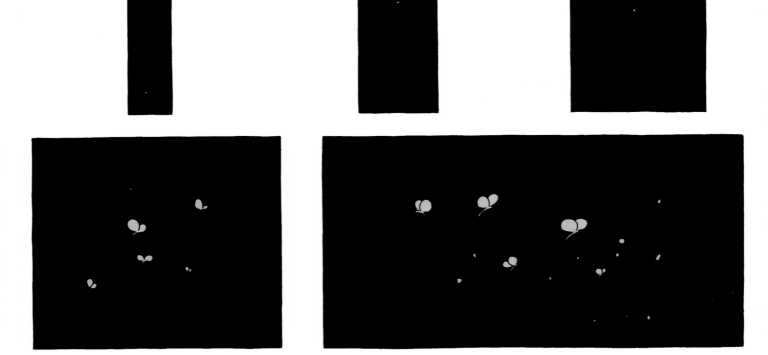

WELL IN A HUNDRED YEARS FROM NOW
THEY WILL ATTEMPT TO TELL US HOW

A SCIENTIFIC MEANS TO BLISS
WILL SUPERCEDE THE HUMAN KISS

A SUB ATOMIC CHAIN
WILL MAYBE GALVANIZE THE BRAIN
A BIOCHEMIC TRANCE
WILL ELIMINATE ROMANCE

BUT WHY EVER SHOULD WE CARE WHEN THERE ARE ARROWS IN THE AIR
FORMED BY LOVERS' ANCIENT ART THAT GO STRAIGHT TO MY HEART

A FUTURE SUGAR COATED PILL WOULD GIVE OUR LOVERS TIME TO KILL
I THINK THEY'RE WORKING FAR TOO MUCH FOR THE REDUNDANCY OF TOUCH

BUT WHAT WILL MAKE ME YOURS ARE A MILLION DEADLY SPORES
FORMED BY LOVERS' ANCIENT ART THAT GO STRAIGHT TO MY HEART

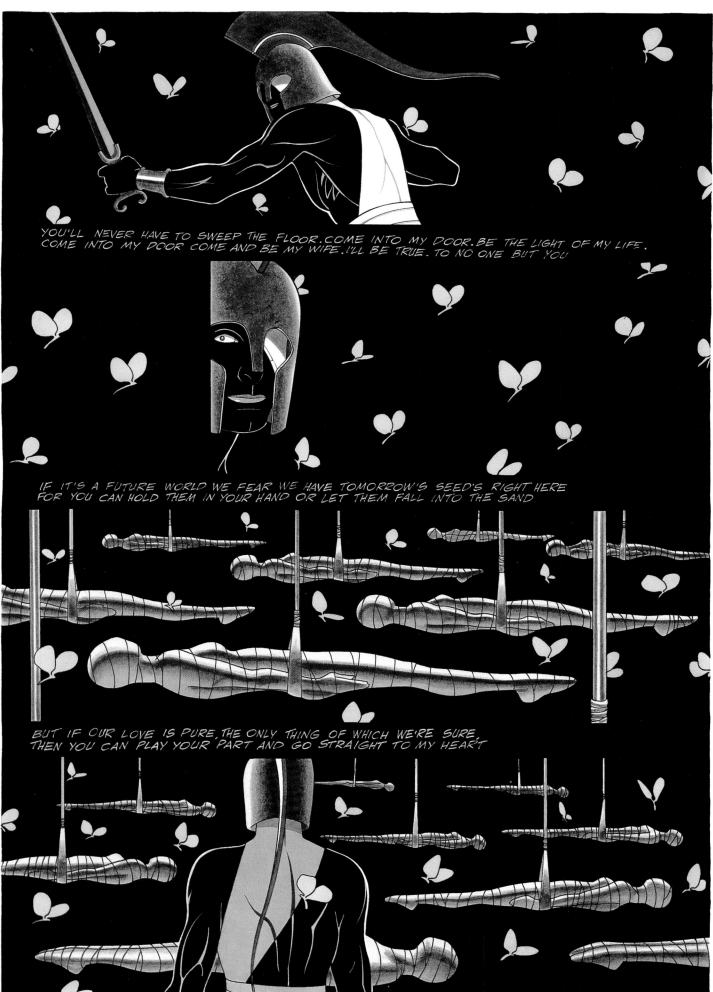

YOU'LL NEVER HAVE TO SWEEP THE FLOOR. COME INTO MY DOOR. BE THE LIGHT OF MY LIFE.
COME INTO MY DOOR COME AND BE MY WIFE. I'LL BE TRUE. TO NO ONE BUT YOU

IF IT'S A FUTURE WORLD WE FEAR WE HAVE TOMORROW'S SEED'S RIGHT HERE
FOR YOU CAN HOLD THEM IN YOUR HAND OR LET THEM FALL INTO THE SAND

BUT IF OUR LOVE IS PURE, THE ONLY THING OF WHICH WE'RE SURE,
THEN YOU CAN PLAY YOUR PART AND GO STRAIGHT TO MY HEAR'T

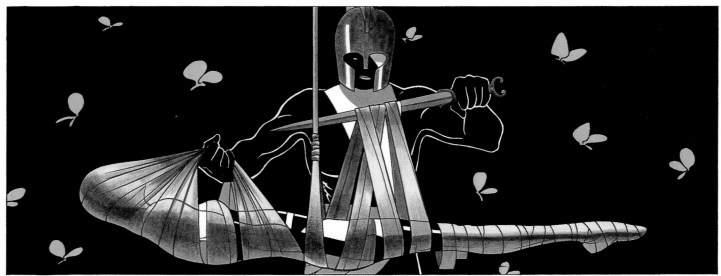

IF I SHOULD SEEK IMMUNITY AND LOVE YOU WITH IMPUNITY THEN THE ONLY THING TO DO

IS FOR ME TO PLEDGE MYSELF TO YOU. BUT THEY ONLY DEALT ONE CARD, SO FOR ME IT IS NOT HARD.

YOU'RE THE BRIGHT STAR IN MY CHART

YOU GO STRAIGHT TO MY HEART
COME INTO MY DOOR
BE THE LIGHT OF MY LIFE
COME INTO MY DOOR
YOU'LL NEVER HAVE TO SWEEP THE FLOOR
COME INTO MY DOOR
BE THE LIGHT OF MY LIFE
COME INTO MY DOOR
COME AND BE MY WIFE
I'LL BE TRUE . TO NO ONE BUT YOU

43

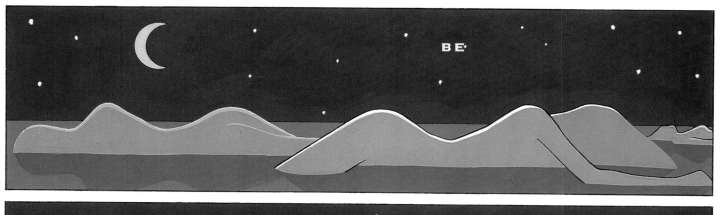

BE·

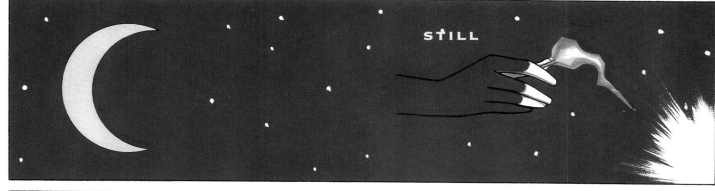

STILL

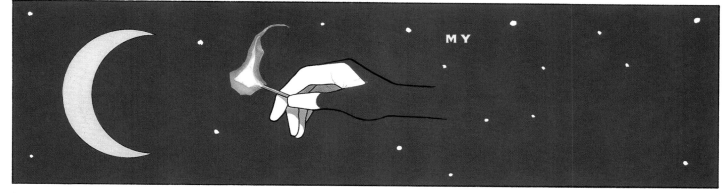

MY

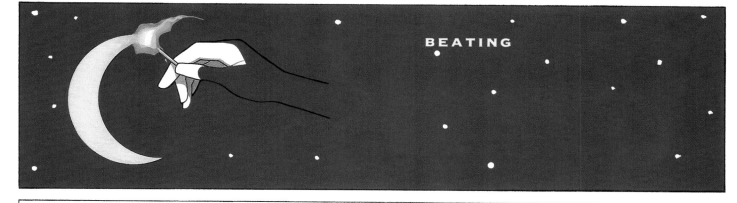

BEATING

HEART

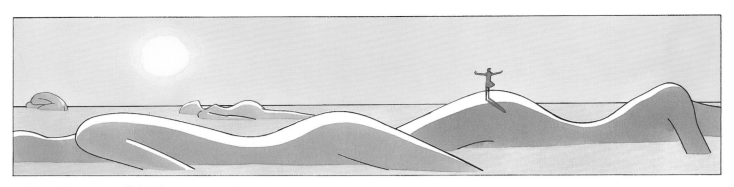

BE STILL MY BEATING HEART
IT WOULD BE BETTER TO BE COOL

IT'S NOT TIME TO BE OPEN JUST YET
A LESSON ONCE LEARNED IS SO HARD TO FORGET

BE STILL MY BEATING HEART
OR I'LL BE TAKEN FOR A FOOL

IT'S NOT HEALTHY TO RUN AT THIS PACE
THE BLOOD RUNS SO RED TO MY FACE

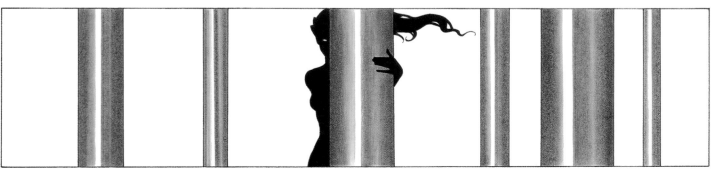

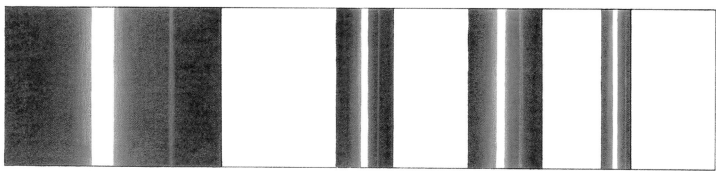

I'VE BEEN TO EVERY SINGLE BOOK I KNOW
TO SOOTHE THE THOUGHTS THAT PLAGUE ME SO

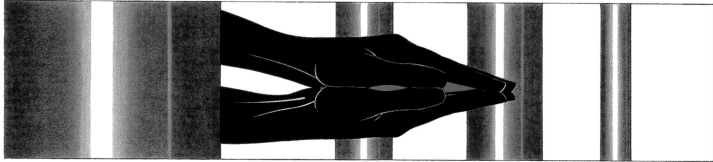

I SINK LIKE A STONE THAT'S BEEN THROWN IN THE OCEAN
MY LOGIC HAS DROWNED IN A SEA OF EMOTION

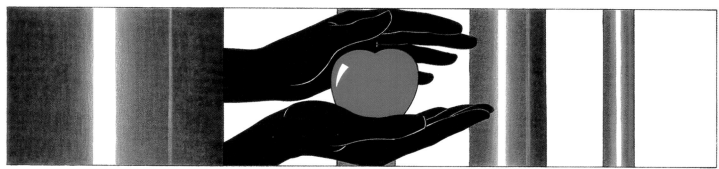

STOP BEFORE YOU START
BE STILL MY BEATING HEART

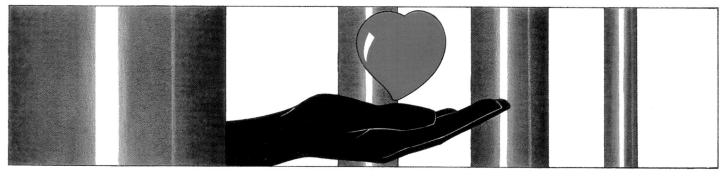

RESTORE MY BROKEN DREAMS
SHATTERED LIKE A FALLING GLASS

I'M NOT READY TO BE BROKEN JUST YET. A LESSON ONCE LEARNED IS SO HARD TO FORGET. BE STILL MY BEATING HEART

YOU MUST LEARN TO STAND YOUR GROUND. IT'S NOT HEALTHY TO RUN AT THIS PACE THE BLOOD RUNS SO RED TO MY FACE

I'VE BEEN TO EVERY SINGLE BOOK I KNOW TO SOOTHE THE THOUGHTS THAT PLAGUE ME SO

STOP BEFORE YOU START BE STILL MY BEATING HEART

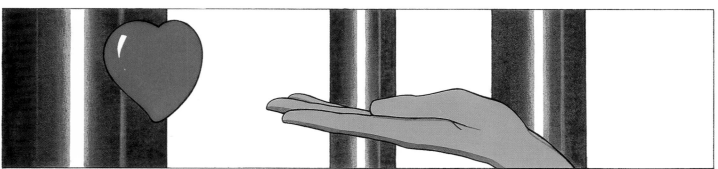

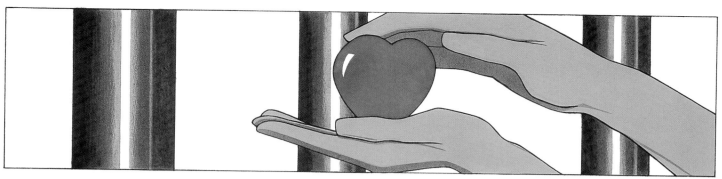

NEVER TO BE WRONG
NEVER TO MAKE PROMISES THAT BREAK

IT'S LIKE SINGING IN THE WIND. OR WRITING ON THE SURFACE OF A LAKE
AND I WRIGGLE LIKE A FISH CAUGHT ON DRY LAND

AND I STRUGGLE TO AVOID ANY HELP AT HAND

I SINK LIKE A STONE THAT'S BEEN THROWN IN THE OCEAN
MY LOGIC HAS DROWNED IN A SEA OF EMOTION

STOP BEFORE YOU START. BE STILL MY BEATING HEART

ROCK STEADY

WORDS

STING

ART

ENEA RIBOLDI

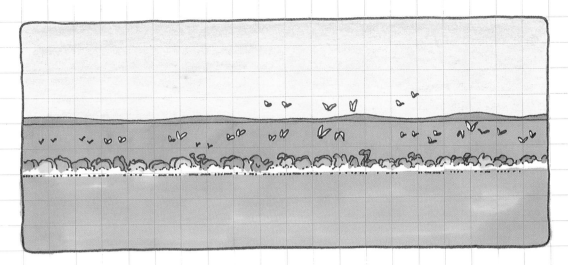

SAW AN AD IN THE NEWSPAPER THAT CAUGHT MY EYE. I SAID TO MY BABY:

THIS SOUNDS LIKE THE TICKET FOR YOU AND I

IT SAID VOLUNTEERS WANTED FOR A VERY SPECIAL TRIP TO COMMUNE WITH MOTHER NATURE ON A BIG WOODEN SHIP

WE TOOK A TAXI TO THE RIVER IN CASE ANY PLACES WERE FREE

THERE WAS AN OLD GUY WITH A BEARD AND EVERY KIND OF CREATURE AS FAR AS THE EYE COULD SEE

THIS OLD GUY WAS THE BOSS, HE SAID:

HE SAID: HE'D HEARD GOD'S MESSAGE ON THE RADIO IT WAS GOING TO RAIN FOREVER AND HE'D TOLD HIM TO GO

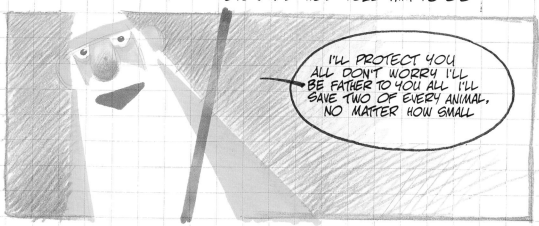

51

IT RAINED FOR FORTY DAYS AND FORTY LONG NIGHTS

I'D NEVER SEEN RAIN LIKE IT AND IT LOOKED LIKE OUR OLD FRIEND
WAS BEING PROVED RIGHT

WE HAD NO TIME TO WORRY THOUGH THERE WAS JUST TOO
MUCH TO DO BETWEEN THE SIGNIFIED MONKEY AND THE KANGAROO

WE HAD TO WASH ALL THE ANIMALS WE HAD TO FEED THEM TOO
WE WERE MERELY HUMAN SLAVES IN A BIG FLOATING ZOO

WOKE UP THIS MORNING AND SOMETHING HAD CHANGED LIKE A
ROOM IN MY HOUSE HAD JUST BEEN REARRANGED SHE SAID.

IT'S STOPPED
RAINING AND I KNOW
THE GUY'S KIND

BUT IF WE
STAY HERE
MUCH LONGER

I'M GONNA
LOSE MY
MIND.

SO WE SAID WE HAD A MISSION FOR HIS FAVORITE DOVE

TO SEE IF THERE WAS ANY MERCY FROM THIS GREAT GOD ABOVE

SO TO FIND DRY LAND, AWAY THE WHITE BIRD FLEW WE DIDN'T
NEED NO COUNTRY JUST A ROCK WOULD DO

WHEN THE DOVE CAME BACK TO US, HE THREW DOWN A TWIG
IT WAS MANNA FROM HEAVEN AND MEANT WE COULD BLOW THIS GIG.

GLIGOROV   STING

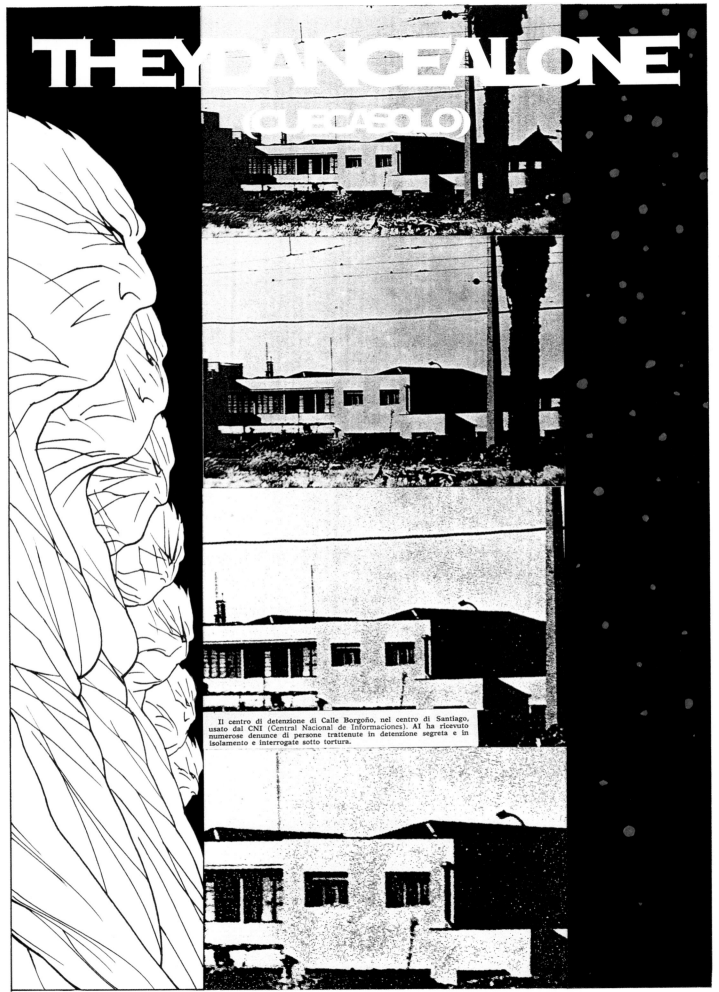

THEY DANCE ALONE
(CUECA SOLO)

Il centro di detenzione di Calle Borgoño, nel centro di Santiago, usato dal CNI (Central Nacional de Informaciones). AI ha ricevuto numerose denunce di persone trattenute in detenzione segreta e in isolamento e interrogate sotto tortura.

WHY ARE THESE WOMEN HERE DANCING ON THEIR OWN?
WHY IS THERE THIS SADNESS IN THEIR EYES?
WHY ARE THE SOLDIERS HERE
THEIR FACES FIXED LIKE STONE?
I CAN'T SEE WHAT IT IS THAT THEY DESPISE
THEY'RE DANCING WITH THE MISSING
THEY'RE DANCING WITH THE DEAD
THEY DANCE WITH THE INVISIBLE ONES
THEIR ANGUISH IS UNSAID
THEY'RE DANCING WITH THEIR FATHERS
THEY'RE DANCING WITH THEIR SONS
THEY'RE DANCING WITH THEIR HUSBANDS
THEY DANCE ALONE

Troops patrol Santiago on 1 May 1986. By the end of the day, which saw non-violent protests throughout Chile, at least one person had been shot dead, many wounded and over a thousand arrested in Santiago alone. Eight people died during similar protests on 2 and 3 July 1986.

THEY DANCE ALONE
IT'S THE ONLY FORM OF
PROTEST THEY'RE ALLOWED
I'VE SEEN THEIR SILENT FACES
SCREAM SO LOUD
IF THEY WERE TO SPEAK THESE
WORDS
THEY'D GO MISSING TOO
ANOTHER WOMAN ON THE
TORTURE TABLE
WHAT ELSE CAN THEY DO
THEY'RE DANCING WITH THE MISSING
THEY'RE DANCING WITH THE DEAD
THEY DANCE WITH THE INVISIBLE
ONES
THEIR ANGUISH IS UNSAID

THEY'RE DANCING WITH
THEIR FATHERS
THEY'RE DANCING WITH
THEIR SONS
THEY'RE DANCING WITH
THEIR HUSBANDS
THEY DANCE ALONE

Diana AARON Sviglsky (journalist)

Guillermo BEAUSIRE Alonso (engineer)

Migue[l] Casti[...]

Rene Roberto ACUÑA Reyes (student)

Jose Domingo ADASME Nunez (farmworker)

Arturo [...] (paint[...])

Francisco Eduardo AEDO Carrasco (architect)

Nalvia Rosa ALVARADO Mena (housewife)

Wash[...] (pri[...])

Maria Angelica ANDREOLI Bravo (secretary)

Antonio AGUIRRE Vasquez (carpenter)

Pedr[...] (wor[...])

Dynaldo H ARANEDA Pizzini (student)

Maria ARRIAGADA Jerez (primary school teacher)

Artu[...] (tea[...])

THEY DANCE ALONE
ONE DAY WE'LL DANCE
ON THEIR GRAVES
ONE DAY WE'LL SING
OUR FREEDOM
ONE DAY WE'LL LAUGH
IN OUR JOY
AND WE'LL DANCE
ONE DAY WE'LL DANCE
ON THEIR GRAVES
ONE DAY WE'LL SING
OUR FREEDOM
ONE DAY WE'LL LAUGH
IN OUR JOY
AND WE'LL DANCE

Arturo BARRIA Araneda (teacher)

Jose Luis, BAEZA Cruces (trader)

Mari[...] Tapi[...]

Pablo Ramon ARANDA Schmidt (medical student)

Ruben David ARROYO Padilla (white collar worker)

Luis CALF[...] (hos[...])

Maria Isabel BELTRAN Sanchez (music student)

Jose Ramon ASCENCIO Subiabre (artisan)

Jose Braulio ASTORGA Nanjari (carpenter)

Osvaldo CERNA Huard (accountant)

Amelia BRUH (interior de

Jaime BUZIO Lorca (biology student)

Alvaro BARRIOS Duque (student of english)

Carlos Alberto CARRASCO Matus (military service)

Eduardo A CAMPOS Barra (Mechanic)

Enrique CAR (agronomy s

Manuel Edgardo CORTES Joo (book-keeper)

Juan Segundo CORTEZ Cortez (worker)

Domingo CUBILLOS Guajardo (worker)

Pedro CURIHUAN Paillan (farmworker)

Ivan INSUN (medical d

Jorge H D'ORIVAL Briceno (veterinary surgeon)

Luis Eduardo DURAN Rivas (student of journalism)

Martin ELGUETA Pinto (economics student)

Antonio ELIZONDO Ormaechea (engineer)

Horacio N CARAVANTE (travelli

ELLAS DANZAN CON LOS DESAPARECIDOS
ELLAS DANZAN CON LOS MUERTOS
ELLAS DANZAN CON AMORES INVISIBLES
ELLAS DANZAN CON SILENCIOSA ANGUSTIA
DANZAN CON SUS PADRES
DANZAN CON SUS HIJOS
DANZAN CON SUS ESPOSOS
ELLAS DANZAN SOLAS
DANZAN SOLAS

Rodolfo ESPEJO Gomez (business student)

Juan IBARRA Toledo (student of social work)

Jose HERRERA Villegas (high school student)

Maria Teresa ELTIT Contreras (student of social work)

Luis Carlos Cortes (commercial

Muriel DOCKENDORF Navarrete (sociology student)

Bernardo DE CASTRO Lopez (commercial artist)

Felix DE LA JARA Goyeneche (history student)

Alfonso Rene CHANFREAU Oyarce (philosophy student)

Juan Rosend Olivares (veterinary

Gaston CIFUENTES Norambuena (trader)

Brothers: Jorge E. & Juan C. ANDRONICOS Antequera (students)

Jacqueline del Carmen BINFA Contreras (secretary)

Alejandro Luis AVALOS Davidson (university lecturer)

Jose Ignacio Maldonado (farmworker)

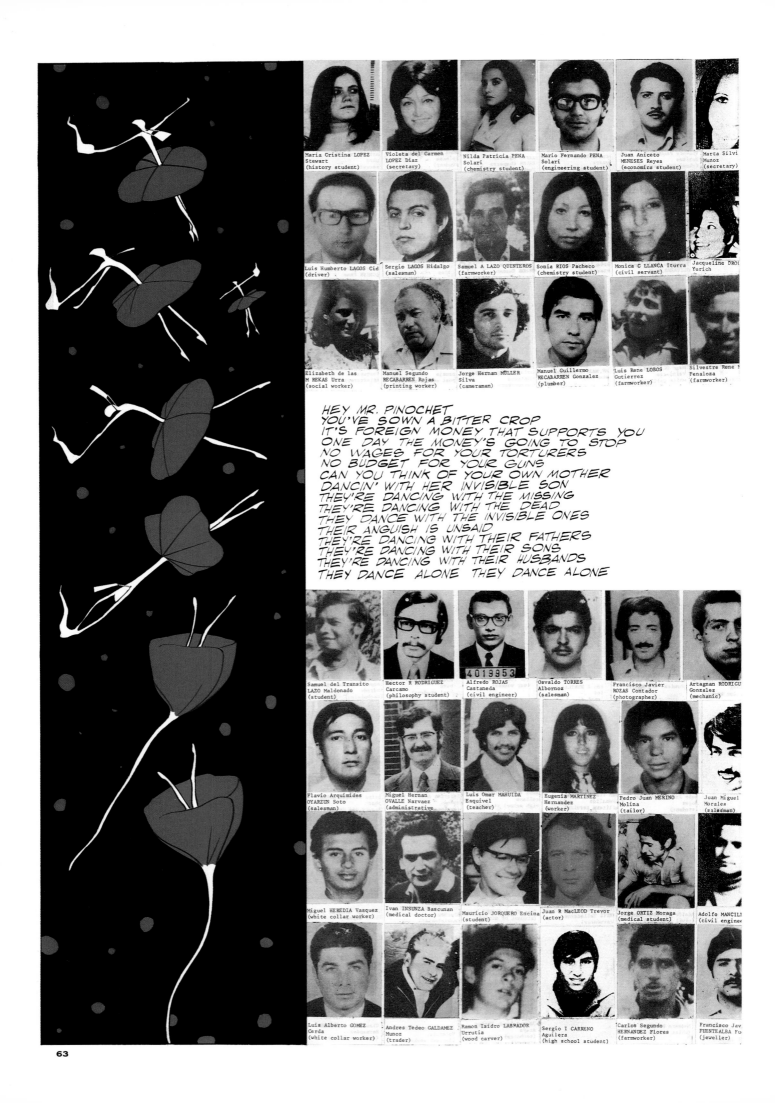

Maria Cristina LOPEZ
Stewart
(history student)

Violeta del Carmen
LOPEZ Diaz
(secretary)

Nilda Patricia PENA
Solari
(chemistry student)

Mario Fernando PENA
Solari
(engineering student)

Juan Aniceto
MENESES Reyes
(economics student)

Marta Silvi
Munoz
(secretary)

Luis Humberto LAGOS Cid
(driver)

Sergio LAGOS Hidalgo
(salesman)

Samuel A LAZO QUINTEROS
(farmworker)

Sonia RIOS Pacheco
(chemistry student)

Monica C LLANCA Iturra
(civil servant)

Jacqueline DRO
Yurich

Elizabeth de las
M REKAS Urra
(social worker)

Manuel Segundo
RECABARREN Rojas
(printing worker)

Jorge Hernan MULLER
Silva
(cameraman)

Manuel Guillermo
RECABARREN Gonzalez
(plumber)

Luis Rene LOBOS
Gutierrez
(farmworker)

Silvestre Rene
Penaloza
(farmworker)

HEY MR. PINOCHET
YOU'VE SOWN A BITTER CROP
IT'S FOREIGN MONEY THAT SUPPORTS YOU
ONE DAY THE MONEY'S GOING TO STOP
NO WAGES FOR YOUR TORTURERS
NO BUDGET FOR YOUR GUNS
CAN YOU THINK OF YOUR OWN MOTHER
DANCIN' WITH HER INVISIBLE SON
THEY'RE DANCING WITH THE MISSING
THEY'RE DANCING WITH THE DEAD
THEY DANCE WITH THE INVISIBLE ONES
THEIR ANGUISH IS UNSAID
THEY'RE DANCING WITH THEIR FATHERS
THEY'RE DANCING WITH THEIR SONS
THEY'RE DANCING WITH THEIR HUSBANDS
THEY DANCE ALONE THEY DANCE ALONE

Samuel del Transito
LAZO Maldonado
(student)

Hector R RODRIGUEZ
Carcamo
(philosophy student)

Alfredo ROJAS
Castaneda
(civil engineer)

Osvaldo TORRES
Albornoz
(salesman)

Francisco Javier
ROZAS Contador
(photographer)

Artagnan RODRIGU
Gonzalez
(mechanic)

Flavio Arquimides
OYARZUN Soto
(salesman)

Miguel Hernan
OVALLE Narvaez
(administrative

Luis Omar MAHUIDA
Esquivel
(teacher)

Eugenia MARTINEZ
Hernandez
(worker)

Pedro Juan MERINO
Molina
(tailor)

Juan Miguel
Morales
(salesman)

Miguel HEREDIA Vasquez
(white collar worker)

Ivan INSUNZA Bascunan
(medical doctor)

Mauricio JORQUERO Encina
(student)

Juan R MacLEOD Trevor
(actor)

Jorge ORTIZ Moraga
(medical student)

Adolfo MANCILL
(civil enginee

Luis Alberto GOMEZ
Cerda
(white collar worker)

Andres Tedeo GALDAMEZ
Munoz
(trader)

Ramon Isidro LABRADOR
Urrutia
(wood carver)

Sergio I CARRENO
Aguilera
(high school student)

Carlos Segundo
HERNANDEZ Flores
(farmworker)

Francisco Jav
FUENTEALBA Fu
(jeweller)

Bautista VON SCHOUWEN Vasey (surgeon)

Victor Julio VIVANCO Vasquez (student)

Hector Patricio VERGARA Doxrud (civil engineer)

Ricardo Manuel WEIBEL Navarrete (driver)

Ida Amelia VERA Almarza (architect)

Jose Manuel RAMIREZ Rosales (artisan)

Ernesto Guillermo SALAMANCA Morales (philosophy student)

Jose del Carmen SAGREDO Pacheco (carpenter)

Oscar Humberto HERNANDEZ Flores (farmworker)

Ariel Martin SALINAS Argomedo (sociology student)

Sergio Daniel TORMEN Mendez (cyclist)

Carlos Ramon RIOSECO Espinoza (salesman)

Agustin Eduardo REYES Gonzalez (art student)

Julio F TAPIA Martinez (driver)

Juan Luis RIVERA Matus (electricity company)

Sergio RIVERAS Villavicencio (white collar worker)

Patricio Antonio SOTO Cerna (carpenter)

Luis Dagoberto SAN MARTIN Vergara (student)

Claudio VENEGAS Lazzaro (high school student)

Jaime Eugenio ROBOTHAM Bravo (sociology student)

Luis Ramon SILVA Carreno (farmworker)

Fernando Guillermo SILVA Camus (interior decorator)

Dixon RETAMAL Cornejo (student)

Oscar Enrique VALLADARES Caroca (farmworker)

Marcos QUINONEZ Lembach (white collar worker)

Jose Orlando FLORES Araya (technical high school student)

Claudio E CONTRERAS Hernandez (civil engineer)

Manuel Jesus VILLALOBOS Diaz (sociology student)

Sergio Alfonso REYES Navarrete (engineer)

Daniel Abraham REYES Pina (hair-dresser)

Carlos Eladio SALCEDO Morales (trader)

Alfredo Ernesto SALINAS Vasquez (plasterer)

Rodolfo Antonio MAUREIRA Munoz (farmworker)

Francisco Javier FUENTEALBA Fuentealba (jeweller)

Jorge Enrique ESPINOZA Mendez (philosophy student)

Hernan SARMIENTO Sabater (medical student)

Guillermo GONZALEZ de Asis (bricklayer)

Sergio Alejandro RIFFO Ramos (student)

Carlos Enriquez SANCHEZ Cornejo (post office worker)

Jose Caupolican VILLAGRA Astudillo (municipal worker)

Jose Alfredo VIDAL Molina (employee of ECA -

Ramon Osvaldo NUNEZ Espinoza (student)

Gilberto P URBINA Chamorro (medical student)

Enrique TORO Romero (railway worker)

Antonio Sergio CABEZAS Quijada (civil servant)

Rodolfo Valentin GONZALEZ Perez (weaver)

Jose Alberto SALAZAR Aguilera (student of social

Abel Alfredo VILCHES Figueroa (panel beater)

Juan Rene MOLINA Mogollones (worker)

Eduardo F MIRANDA Lobos (topographer)

Jorge OLIVARES Graindorge (white collar worker)

Silvestre Rene MUNOZ Penaloza (farmworker)

Octavio Julio ETTIGER

Jose Enrique CORVALAN Valencia (factory worker)

Hector GONZALEZ Fernandez (white collar worker)

Andres PEREIRA Salsberg (agricultural technician)

Agustin Almiro MARTINEZ Meza (mechanical engineer)

Anselmo RADRIGAN Plaza (computer student)

Daniel PALMA Robledo (ecologist)

Hus... J...

Eduardo ...rales (...ruction worker)

So... Mercedes ... Reyes (...tary)

Gerardo SILVA Saldivar (student)

Hernan SARMIENTO Sabater (medical student)

Juan Carlos PERELMAN Ide (engineer)

Carlos Fredy PEREZ Vargas (commercial artist)

Luis Jaime PALOMINOS Rojas (student)

Juan Francisco PENA Fuenzalida (military service)

Fernando de la Cruz OLIVARES Mori (United Nations)

Alan Roberto BRUCE Catalan (engineering student)

Leopoldo Daniel MUNOZ Andrade (technician)

Jose Fidel FLORES Perez (student of mining technology)

Maria J RAMIREZ Gallegos (actress)

Isidro PIZARRO Meniconi (IBM technician)

Vicente PALOMINOS Benitez (chemistry teacher)

Gary Nelson OLMOS Guzman (trader)

Husband & Wife: Edwin VAN YURICK Altamirano

Jorge Isaac FUE... Alarcon (sociologist)

Cecilia M BOJANIC Abad (book keeper)

Artemio Segundo GUTIERREZ Avila (jeweller)

Edgardo Agustin MORALES Chaparro (plumber)

SET E

THEM

FREE

65

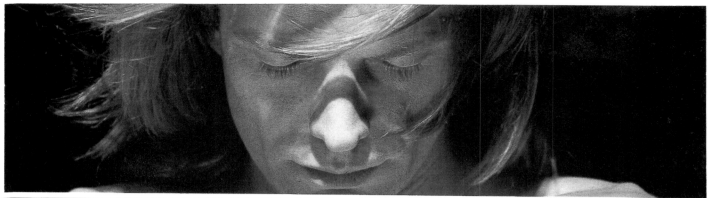

FREE, FREE
SET THEM FREE

FREE, FREE SET
THEM FREE
FREE, FREE SET
THEM FREE

67 FREE, FREE SET
THEM FREE

IF YOU NEED
SOMEBODY, CALL
MY NAME
IF YOU WANT
SOMEONE, YOU CAN
DO THE SAME
IF YOU WANT
TO KEEP
SOMETHING
PRECIOUS
YOU GOT TO LOCK
IT UP AND THROW
AWAY THE KEY
IF YOU WANT TO
HOLD ONTO YOUR
POSSESSION
DON'T EVEN
THINK ABOUT ME
IF YOU LOVE
SOMEBODY, SET
THEM FREE

IF IT'S A
MIRROR YOU
WANT, JUST
LOOK INTO
MY EYES
OR A WHIPPING
BOY, SOMEONE
TO DESPISE
OR A PRISONER
IN THE DARK
TIED UP IN
CHAINS YOU
JUST CAN'T SEE

OR A BEAST IN A
GILDED CAGE
THAT'S ALL SOME
PEOPLE EVER
WANT TO BE
IF YOU LOVE
SOMEBODY, SET
THEM FREE

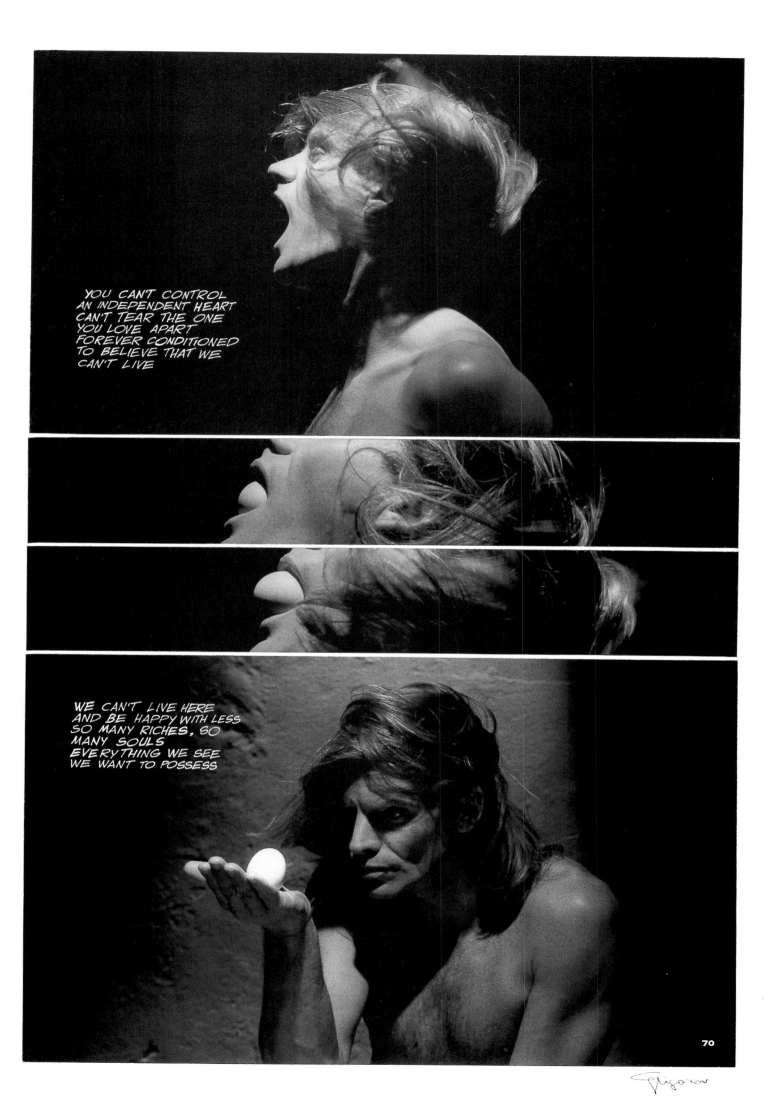

YOU CAN'T CONTROL
AN INDEPENDENT HEART
CAN'T TEAR THE ONE
YOU LOVE APART
FOREVER CONDITIONED
TO BELIEVE THAT WE
CAN'T LIVE

WE CAN'T LIVE HERE
AND BE HAPPY WITH LESS
SO MANY RICHES, SO
MANY SOULS
EVERYTHING WE SEE
WE WANT TO POSSESS

IF YOU NEED SOMEBODY, CALL MY NAME IF YOU WANT SOMEONE, YOU CAN DO THE SAME

IF YOU WANT TO KEEP SOMETHING PRECIOUS YOU GOT TO LOCK IT UP AND THROW AWAY THE KEY

IF YOU WANT TO HOLD ONTO YOUR POSSESSION DON'T EVEN THINK ABOUT ME

IF YOU LOVE SOMEBODY, SET THEM FREE

CHILDREN'S CRUSADE

Young men, soldiers,
nineteen fourteen,
marching through
countries they'd
never seen.
Virgins with rifles, a
game of charades
all for a children's
crusade.
Pawns in the game
are not victims of chance,
strewn on the fields of
Belgium and France,
poppies for young men,
death's bitter trade, all of
those young lives betrayed.
The children of England
would never be slaves
they're trapped on the whire
and dying in waves, the flower
of England face down in the mud
and stained in the blood of
a whole generation.
Corpulent generals, safe
behind lines, history's
lessons drowned in red wine,
poppies for young men,
death's bitter trade
all of those young lives
betrayed, all for a
children's crusade.
The children of England
would never be slaves,
they're trapped on the
wire and dying in waves,
the flower of England
face down in the mud
and stained in the blood
of a whole generation.
Midnight in Soho, nineteen
eighty four, fixing in
doorways, opium slaves
poppies for young men.
Such bitter trade, all of
those young lives
betrayed, all for a
children's crusade.

ЯUSSIANS

In Europe and America there's a growing feeling of hysteria conditioned to respond to all the threats in the rhetorical speeches of the soviets. Mr. Krushchev said we will bury you I don't subscribe to this point of view. It would be such an ignorant thing to do if the Russians love their children too.

Sting

How can I save my little boy from Oppenheimer's deadly toy. There is no monopoly of common sense on either side of the political fence. We share the same biology regardless of ideology. Believe me when I say to you I hope the Russians love their children too.

There is no historical precedent to put the words in the mouth of the president. There's no such thing as a winnable war. It's a lie we don't believe anymore.

Mr. Reagan said we will protect you. I don't subscribe to this point of view. Believe me when I say to you I hope the Russians love their children too.

We share the same biology regardless of ideology. What might save us me and you. Is that the Russians love their children too.

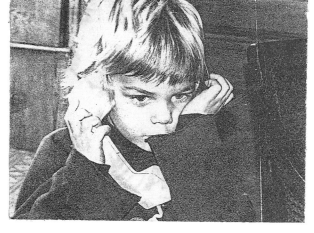

FORTRESS AROUND YOUR HEART

Under the ruins of a walled city
crumbling towers in beams of yellow light
No flags of truce, no cries of pity
The siege guns had been pounding
all through the night
It took a day to build the city
We walked through its streets in the
afternoon
As I returned across the fields I'd known
I recognized the walls that once made
I had to stop in my tracks for fear
Of walking on the mines I'd laid
And if I have built this fortress
Around your heart
Encircled you in trenches and barbed wire
Then let me build a bridge
For I cannot fill the chasm
And let me set the battlements on fire
Then I went off to fight some battle
That I'd invented inside my head
Away so long for years and years
You probably thought or even
Wished that I was dead
While the armies all are sleeping
Beneath the tattered flag we'd made
I had to stop in my tracks for fear
Of walking on the mines I'd laid
This prison has now become your home
A sentence you seem prepared to pay
It took a day to build the city
We walked through its streets
In the afternoon
As I returned across the lands I'd known
I recognized the fields where I'd once played
I had to stop in my tracks for fear
Of walking on the mines I'd laid

WE WORK THE BLACK SEAM TOGETHER

This place has changed for good
your economic theory said it would

it's hard for us to understand
we can't give up our jobs the way we should

our blood has stained the coal
we tunneled deep inside the nations soul

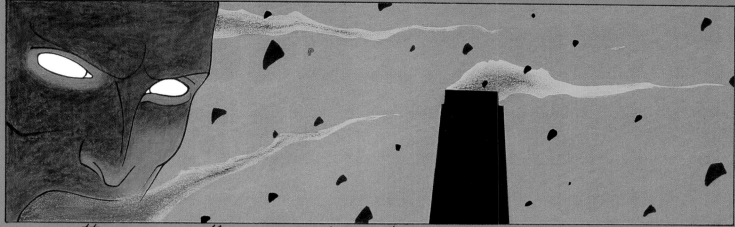

we matter more than pounds and pence
your economic theory makes no sense

one day in a nuclear age they may understand our rage
they build machines that they can't control

and bury the waste in a great big hole
power was to become cheap and clean

grimy faces were never seen
but deadly for twelve thousand years is carbon 14

we work the black seam together
the seam lies underground, 3 million years of pressure packed it

down, we walk through ancient forest lands

and light a thousand cities with our hands.
Your dark satanic mills have made redundant all our mining skills

You can't exchange a six inch band for all the poisoned steams in Cumberland.

One day in a nuclear age they may understand our rage, they build machines that they can't control and bury the waste in a great big hole.

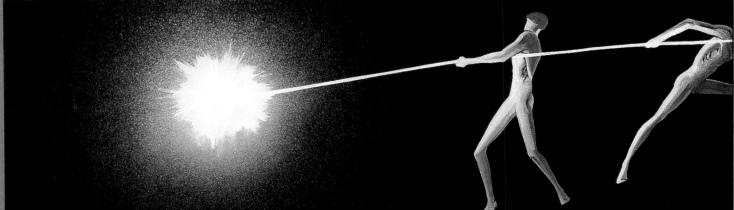

Power was to become cheap and clean grimy faces were never seen.

82

but deadly for twelve thousand years is carbon 14
We work the black seam together

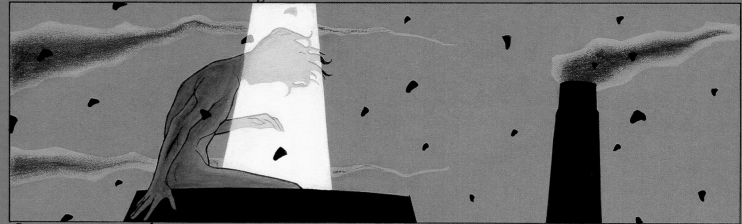

Our conscious lives run deep
You cling onto your mountain while we sleep

This way of life is part of me, there is no price so only let me be and should
the children weep the turning world will sing their souls to sleep

When you have sunk without a trace the universe will suck me into place

One day in a nuclear age they may understand our rage
they build machines that they can't control and bury the waste in a great

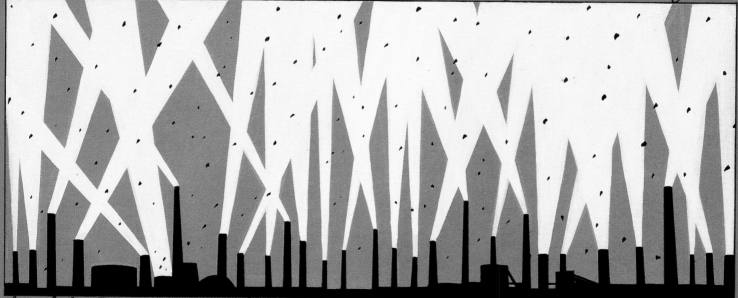

big hole. Power was to become cheap and clean, grimy faces were never seen
but deadly for twelve thousand years is carbon 14

We work the black seam together

THERE'S A **MOON** OVER

BOURBON STREET TONIGHT

I SEE FACES AS THEY **PASS**
BENEATH THE PALE LAMPLIGHT

I'VE NO CHOICE BUT TO **FOLLOW**
THAT CALL

THE BRIGHT **LIGHTS**,

THE PEOPLE,

AND THE MOON AND **ALL**

I PRAY EVERY DAY TO BE STRONG FOR
I KNOW WHAT I **DO** MUST BE WRONG

S

OH YOU'LL NEVER SEE MY **SHADE**

F

OR HEAR THE SOUND OF MY **FEET**

W

WHILE THERE'S A MOON

O

OVER BOURBON STREET

M

IT WAS **MANY** YEARS AGO THAT

I

I BECAME WHAT I AM

T

I WAS **TRAPPED** IN THIS LIFE LIKE AN INNOCENT LAMB

A

NOW I CAN NEVER SHOW MY FACE **AT** NOON

T — AND YOU'LL ONLY SEE ME WALKING BY **THE** LIGHT OF THE MOON

B — THE BRIM OF MY HAT HIDES THE EYE OF A **BEAST**

P — I'VE THE FACE OF A SINNER BUT THE HANDS OF A **PRIEST**

N — OH YOU'LL **NEVER** SEE MY SHADE OR HEAR THE SOUND OF MY FEET WHILE THERE'S A MOON OVER BOURBON ST.

S — **SHE** WALKS EVERYDAY THROUGH THE STREETS OF NEW ORLEANS

Y — SHE'S INNOCENT AND **YOUNG** FROM A FAMILY OF MEANS

W — I HAVE STOOD MANY TIMES OUTSIDE HER **WINDOW** AT NIGHT

I — TO STRUGGLE WITH MY **INSTINCT** IN THE PALE MOONLIGHT

HOW COULD I BE THIS WAY WHEN I PRAY TO GOD ABOVE

I MUST LOVE WHAT I DESTROY

AND DESTROY THE THING I LOVE

OH YOU'LL NEVER SEE MY SHADE

OR HEAR THE SOUND OF MY FEET

WHILE THERE'S A MOON

OVER BOURBON

STREET

Consider me gone

you can't say that
you can't say
you can't
you

There were rooms of forgiveness in the house that we share but the space has been emptied of whatever was there

that say that can't say that

There were cupboards
of patience
There were shelfloads
of care but whoever came
calling found nobody
there

After today
Consider me gone

you
you can't
you can't say
you can't say that

Roses have thorns
and shining waters
mud and cancer lurks
deep in the sweetest bud
clouds and eclipses
stain the moon
and the sun
and history reeks
of the wrongs we
have done

can't say that
say that
that

after today

Consider me gone

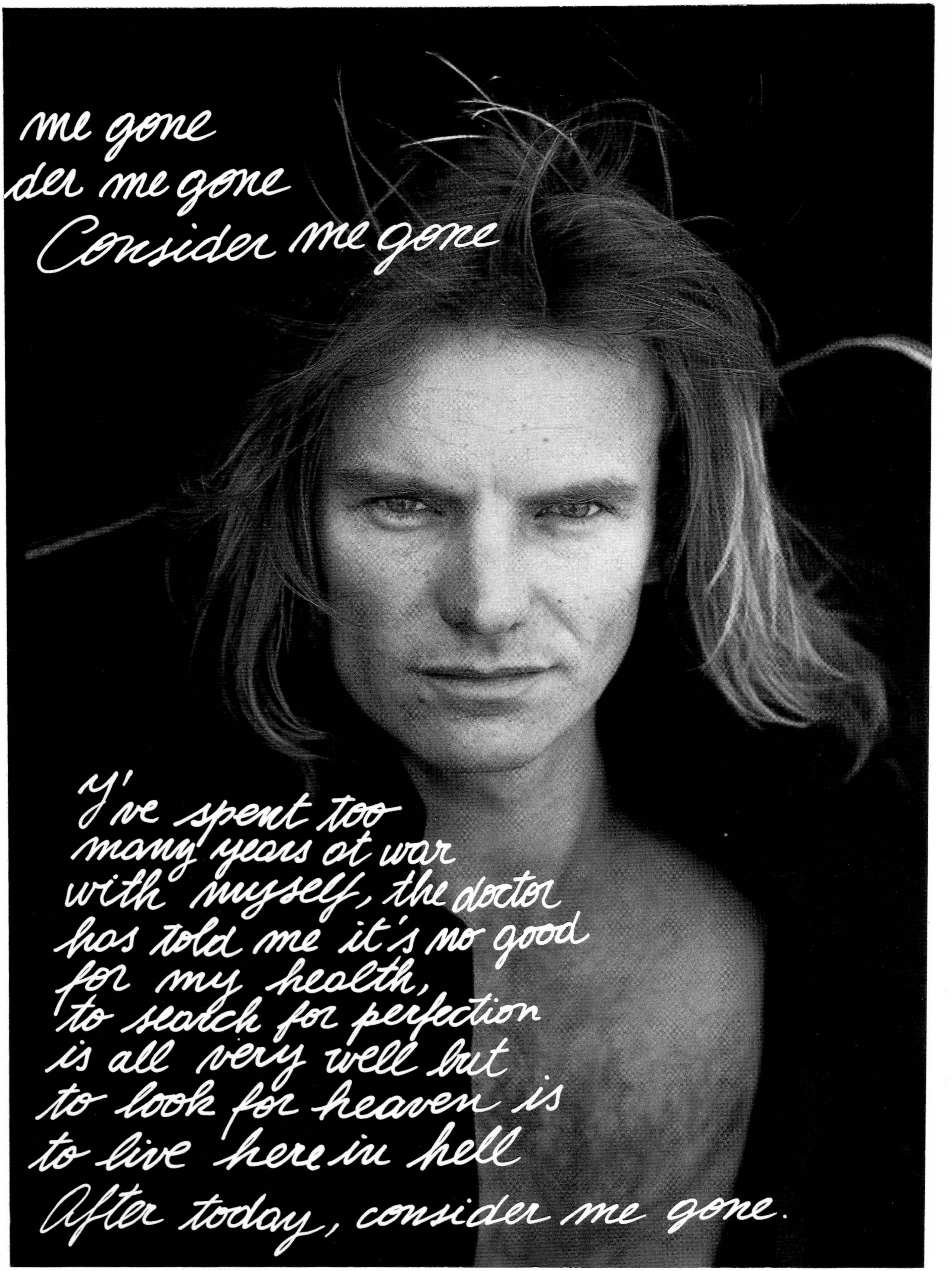

me gone
der me gone
Consider me gone

Y've spent too
many years at war
with myself, the doctor
has told me it's no good
for my health,
to search for perfection
is all very well but
to look for heaven is
to live here in hell
After today, consider me gone.

For high quality T-shirts featuring these designs, send U.S. $20 plus $3.50 for shipping and handling. Specify the shirt number. To order, or for information about other STING merchandise, write to IRS Merchandise at 3939 Lankershim Boulevard, Universal City, California 91604. In England, write Bugle House, 21A Noel Street, London W1V 3PD. In Europe, write: Chateau de Marouatte, Grand Brassac, 24 350 Tocane Saint Apre, France.

S90PT

S90GT

S90FT